Contents

SonGames 2004 Course Overview 2

How to Use This Book 4

Snapshot of SonGames 2004 4
- Course Description 4
- Set the Atmosphere 5
- Winning Ideas 6

Materials Preview 8
- Starter Kit 8
- Director's Sample Pack 8
- Super Decorating & Resource Pack 9
- Music & Skit Production Pack 9
- Super Starter Pack 9

Director's Planning Guide 10
- 1. Plan Your VBS Program 10
  Planning Your Early Childhood VBS 11
- 2. Recruit Your VBS Staff 14
  Using Youth Helpers 17
  Sample Flyers for Staff Recruitment 18
- 3. Train Your VBS Staff 19

- 4. Publicize Your VBS 20
- 5. Evangelism 21
- 6. Follow-Up 21
- Director's Countdown Calendar 22

Special Events 23
- Field Trips 23
- Events at Church 23
- SonGames 2004 Preview Event 24
- Closing Ceremony Closing Program 26

Publicity Guide 27
- Build VBS Interest Within the Church 27
- Reach Out to Children from the Community 27

- SonGames 2004 Publicity Pieces 27
- News Release 28
- Publicity Countdown Calendar 29
- Publicity Materials 29

Activity Center Guide 31
- SonGames Training Center 35
- Bible Memory Verse Center 41
- Bible Story Review Center 47
- Missions and Service Center 53
- Recreation Game Center 61
- Snack Center 65

Appendix A: Intergenerational VBS Guide 71

Appendix B: Backyard Bible School 75

Appendix C: Course Overview— *King James Version* 77

Index 78

VBS Questionnaire 79

How to make clean copies from this book

You may make copies of portions of this book with a clean conscience if
- you (or someone in your organization) are the original purchaser;
- you are using the copies you make for a noncommercial purpose (such as teaching or promoting your ministry) within your church or organization;
- you follow the instructions provided in this book.

However, it is ILLEGAL for you to make copies if

- you are using the material to promote, advertise or sell a product or service other than for ministry fund-raising;
- you are using the material in or on a product for sale; or
- you or your organization are not the original purchaser of this book.

By following these guidelines you help us keep our products affordable.

Thank you,
Gospel Light

Permission to make photocopies of or to reproduce by any other mechanical or electronic means in whole or in part any designated* page, illustration or activity in this book is granted only to the original purchaser and is intended for noncommercial use within a church or other Christian organization. None of the material in this book may be reproduced for any commercial promotion, advertising or sale of a product or service. Sharing of the material in this book with other churches or organizations not owned or controlled by the original purchaser is also prohibited. All rights reserved.

*Pages with the following notation can be legally reproduced:
© 2004 Gospel Light. Permission to photocopy granted. SonGames 2004 *Director's Guidebook*

Scripture quotations are taken from the *Holy Bible, New International Version*®. Copyright © 1973, 1978, 1984 by International Bible Society. Used by permission of Zondervan Publishing House. All rights reserved.

Gospel Light Vacation Bible School

- **Founder**, Henrietta Mears
- **Publisher Emeritus**, William T. Greig
- **Publisher, Children's Curriculum and Resources**, Lynnette Pennings, M.A.
- **Senior Consulting Publisher**, Dr. Elmer L. Towns
- **Managing Editor**, Sheryl Haystead
- **Senior Editor**, Kim Fiano
- **Senior Consulting Editors**, Wesley Haystead, M.S.Ed., Christy Weir
- **Senior Editor, Biblical and Theological Issues**, Bayard Taylor, M.Div.
- **Editor**, Karen McGraw
- **Associate Editor**, Heather Kempton
- **Senior Designer**, Carolyn Thomas
- **Art Director**, Lenndy McCullough
- **Cover Design**, Samantha Hsu
- **Illustrator**, Chizuko Yasuda

© 2004 Gospel Light, Ventura, CA 93006. All rights reserved. Printed in the U.S.A.

Gospel Light's SonGames 2004 Course Overview

Session	Bible Story	Focus	Bible Memory Verse	Craft
1 JOIN IN!	God Picks Paul Acts 9:1-22	**PreK/Kindergarten** God sent Jesus to show His love for me. **Elementary** God wants me to be on His team and, through Jesus, offers me His love and forgiveness.	**PreK/Kindergarten** "God made us and we are his." (See Psalm 100:3.) **Elementary** "Know that the Lord is God. It is he who made us, and we are his; we are his people." Psalm 100:3	**PreK/Kindergarten**— Waving Flag **Primary**— Little League Locker **Middler**— Crumple-Art Sports Ball **Preteen**— All-Star Photo Board **Optional for Elementary:** Team Visors
2 TEAM UP!	God's Team Helps Paul Acts 9:20-30; 11:19-26; 13:1-3	**PreK/Kindergarten** God gives me friends so that we can help each other. **Elementary** God gives me a team so that we can cheer each other on.	**PreK/Kindergarten** "Help each other show love." (See Hebrews 10:24.) **Elementary** "Let us consider how we may spur one another on toward love and good deeds." Hebrews 10:24	**PreK/Kindergarten**— Sports Pack **Primary**— Basket Paul **Middler**— God's Team Foam Finger **Preteen**— Pom-Pom Sports Fan
3 GET STRONG!	Paul Stays Strong Acts 16—18:11	**PreK/Kindergarten** God helps me to obey His Word and do good. **Elementary** God gives me strength to obey His instructions.	**PreK/Kindergarten** "I am quick to obey God's Word." (See Psalm 119:32.) **Elementary** "Strengthen me according to your word. I run in the path of your commands." Psalm 119:28,32	**PreK/Kindergarten**— Counting Sneaker **Primary**— Table-Top Soccer **Middler**— Whirling Athletes Yo-Yo **Preteen**— Get Strong Barbell
4 KEEP ON!	Paul Weathers the Storm Acts 27	**PreK/Kindergarten** God promises to be with me when I am afraid. **Elementary** God promises to help me through tough problems.	**PreK/Kindergarten** "Do not fear, for I am with you." Isaiah 41:10 **Elementary** "Do not fear, for I am with you; do not be dismayed, for I am your God. I will strengthen you and help you." Isaiah 41:10	**PreK/Kindergarten**— Paul's Big Storm **Primary**— Keep On! Discus **Middler**— Free-Throw Toy **Preteen**— Sporty Spiral
5 CELEBRATE!	Paul Reaches His Goal Acts 28	**PreK/Kindergarten** God always loves me and helps me. **Elementary** I can celebrate the good things God gives me as a member of His team.	**PreK/Kindergarten** "Thanks be to God!" 1 Corinthians 15:57 **Elementary** "Thanks be to God! He gives us the victory through our Lord Jesus Christ." 1 Corinthians 15:57	**PreK/Kindergarten**— Salt-Art Fireworks **Primary**— God's Team Trading Cards **Middler**— Beanbag Game Ball **Preteen**— Cereal Box of Champions

© 2004 Gospel Light. Permission to p

Bible Theme: God's Team in Action: Paul's Adventures

Theme Verse: "Thanks be to God! He gives us the victory through our Lord Jesus Christ." 1 Corinthians 15:57

SonGames Training Center	Song	Snack	Recreation Game	Skit
Team Flag Every four years the world pauses to watch a parade of athletes march under a sea of nearly 200 different team flags. Your young athletes will enjoy designing and making their own team flags as they learn about joining the best team of all—God's team!	"Join In!" and "The Lord Is God"	Torch Treats	Super Soccer	**Let the Games Begin!** Excitement builds as athletes from around the world arrive at the Son-Games. During the competitions, Joe Gabbyola, sportscaster for VBSN, will provide viewers exclusive coverage of the athletes from the unusual country of Smallvania—gymnast Tumbelina Turn-over, weight lifter Brutus Liftsalot and runner Stella Swift. But where are they?
Trading Pins No one gets to the Olympics on their own—athletes need the support of coaches, family and teammates. As your kids make and trade pins, they'll learn that following God doesn't mean going it alone either. God gives us a team of fellow believers to cheer each other on!	"Teamwork"	Teammate Munchies	Volleyball Relay	**Team Troubles** Strongman Brutus is feeling anything but strong. Not only is his equipment bag missing, but he's also homesick for his family. When he looks to his teammate Stella for encouragement, she is only concerned about her own training. Will Tumbelina team up with Brutus and help him focus on his upcoming competition?
Exhibition Sport What do you get if you cross a helmet, a hockey puck and a basket? A silly sport and a goofy time! Young athletes will have a blast inventing exhibition sports—and rules for their games. They'll also learn how God helps the members of His team get strong as we follow His instructions every day!	"Get Strong"	Swimmers' Snack	Water Ball	**Tumbelina's Terrible Twist** Congratulations, Brutus! Thanks to following his coach's strict training routine, Brutus wins a bronze medal for weight lifting. Too bad Tumbelina doesn't think she needs to follow her coach's advice. When she makes up her own routine, her chance of getting a medal in the freestyle gymnastics competition looks slim.
Decathlon Discovery Persevering through 10 events, decathletes are some of the best athletes in the world. As your team learns about these amazing athletes, they'll discover something that will help them keep on during tough times—remembering the promises of a loving God.	"Do Not Be Afraid"	Bagel Barbells	Fun-athlon	**Stella's Setback** Injured in a fall during her second race, Stella won't even try running her third race if she can't win. But Tumbelina knows Stella can't give up now. Stella's Smallvanian teammates encourage her to keep on trying. They know that win or lose, Stella will still be a champion.
Celebration Medals As flags are raised, tear-streaked athletes sing their national anthems while millions watch them receive medals. Today your kids will create medals to celebrate something even better than pure gold—the victory we have as members of God's team!	"Thanks Be to God"	Power Smoothies	B-Ball Tag	**A Smallvanian Victory** Stella finally finds her team spirit as she and Brutus help Tumbelina prepare for the gymnastics competition. When Tumbelina wins a medal, despite Joe Gabbyola's grim predictions, the entire Smallvanian team celebrates! But the most important victory they achieve at the SonGames is learning the importance of teamwork.

Course Overview

How to Use This Book

Read and follow the steps below to get the most out of your *Director's Guidebook*.

1. Read the "SonGames 2004 Course Overview" chart (pp. 2-3) and "Snapshot of SonGames 2004" (p. 4) to get a good overview of the VBS course.

2. Spread out all of your VBS materials so that you can see each item. Use the "Materials Preview" beginning on page 8 as a guide as you examine each item.

3. Read the "Director's Planning Guide" beginning on page 10. This guide will walk you through many of the steps involved in planning your VBS program: choosing your format, choosing your learning plan, recruiting staff, publicizing your VBS, evangelism and follow-up.

Use the "Director's Countdown Calendar" provided on page 22 as a guide and develop your own VBS calendar.

4. Photocopy the pages you need to distribute to other VBS leaders. Use the following as a checklist:
- Special Events Coordinator (pp. 23-26)
- Publicity Coordinator (pp. 27-30)

If you are using the Activity Center Learning Plan (see pp. 31-34), then copy pages for the following:
- SonGames Training Center Leader (pp. 35-40)
- Bible Memory Verse Leader (pp. 41-46)
- Bible Story Review Leader (pp. 47-52)
- Missions and Service Leader (pp. 53-60)
- Recreation Game Leader (pp. 61-64)
- Snack Leader (pp. 65-70)

MORE HELP is available to you through www.myvbs.com (included in Super Starter Pack). In addition to providing your church with an instant VBS website, www.myvbs.com provides you with SonGames clip art, an easy-to-use calendar, a budget calculator and additional helps for recruitment, training and publicizing your VBS. Visit www.myvbs.com to find out more.

Snapshot of

Course Description

God's Team in Action: Paul's Adventures

The day has finally arrived! Athletes and spectators from around the world are gathering for the most exciting event of the year—the SonGames! International teams proudly carry their flags as they march into the stadium. The crowd cheers at the colorful spectacle, anticipating the amazing days to come. Your children will be thrilled to be part of the excitement as they discover they can all be members of God's team—people worldwide who love and obey Him.

Kids love being part of a team! That's why every activity at SonGames is full of action and camaraderie. Children will cheer each other on as they play outdoor sports just like the Olympians. They'll build team spirit as they design team flags and trade pins with new friends. Through global games, international snacks and gold-medal crafts, kids will learn about the Olympic Games, past and present. They'll also be fascinated to meet one of God's most valuable players, Paul, who lived during the days of the ancient Olympics.

Each day at SonGames children will learn from Paul's example. Through the story of Paul's conversion, they'll learn that Jesus makes it possible for everyone to "Join In!" and be a member of God's team. Children will want to "Team Up!" with encouraging friends when they hear how Paul's friends helped and encouraged him. They'll find God helps them "Get Strong!" and do what's right, as they witness Paul's obedience as he traveled through Greece. Your team will be inspired to "Keep On!" trusting God during tough times, as they watch Paul's perseverance. Lastly, your team will enjoy seeing Paul reach his goal and will "Celebrate!" the many good things that God does for the members of His team!

So begin training now for the biggest event of the year! Go the distance, give it your best shot, and take a giant leap of faith. And remember Paul's words as you prepare to train and strengthen God's young team:

> Thanks be to God! He gives us the victory through our Lord Jesus Christ (1 Corinthians 15:57).

SonGames 2004

Set the Atmosphere

Add an unforgettable dimension to your VBS by filling your church with the sights and sounds of SonGames.

Scenery

Use the patterns and ideas in the *Teaching and Decorating Resources* books and the *Preview Video* to decorate classrooms and activity centers. Clip art is available on our website, www.gospellight.com, or at www.myvbs.com. Give your rooms or centers names appropriate for SonGames: The Stadium (Assembly Hall) for Opening and Closing Assemblies and Skits, Heroes Hall for Bible Story/Life Application Center, SonGames Training Center for Theme Center. Other centers could be called Swimming Arena, Gymnastics Arena, "Nations of the World" Houses, Playing Field, Locker Room, Sports Center, etc.

The Stadium

Heroes Hall

SonGames Training Center

"Nations of the World" Houses

Sounds

The *SonGames* cassette and CD provide lively songs to help your students learn Bible truths. These memorable songs help students and adults alike learn about being members of God's team.

Fun Days

Enlist the help of your VBS students to help set the stage for your VBS. Each day of your VBS, ask students to bring in or wear items to enhance the sporty atmosphere. Consider doing one or more of the following:

⚽ **Sports or International Hat Day** Students and VBS workers wear fun, funny and fantastic hats that they bring from home or that they make at VBS using a variety of art supplies.

⚽ **Funny Hair Day** Encourage everyone involved in your VBS program to come up with his or her most outrageous hairstyle.

5

⚽ **Sports Clothing** Ask students and VBS workers to wear sports-themed clothing one day. Or devote each day to a different sport. Everyone wears clothing and/or carries equipment appropriate for that sport.

⚽ **Color of the Day** Using each day's Motto Pennant as a guide or the color of your choice, students and VBS workers wear the color of the day in their clothing or even their hair!

Staff Names and Group Names

Head Coach: Director
Coach: Bible Teachers, Activity Center Leaders, Guides
Trainers: Youth Helpers

Group your students by

⚽ **Countries:** Romania, Singapore, Denmark, Brazil, etc.

⚽ **Sports:** Rapid Runners, Super Swimmers, Daring Divers, Brilliant B-Ballers, etc.

⚽ **Both of the above:** Romanian Runners, Singapore Swimmers, Danish Divers, Brazilian B-Ballers, etc.

Winning Ideas

Use these extra fun, theme-related ideas to create enthusiasm and excitement for your VBS.

Transitions

When deciding on a way to signal transition times in your schedule, consider the following ideas:

⚽ A designated runner holds a torch aloft as he or she runs around your church campus blowing a whistle.

⚽ Blow an airhorn.

⚽ Over a loudspeaker have an announcer say, "Get ready. Get set. Go!"

Kids in Action

Find kids in your church or community who play and/or are in training for different sports. With the permission of their parents, take photos of the kids in action and use photos to make a bulletin-board collage, to make an album on your church's website, to create a slide-show program or to use in promotional materials for your VBS. During the Opening Assembly, interview the kids or show previously videotaped interviews. Ask them questions about where they train, who helps them train, what they enjoy about their sports and what are the hardest things about their sports.

Official Motto

The official motto for the Olympic Games is "Faster, Higher, Stronger." Develop a motto of your own for your VBS. At the beginning and end of each opening and closing assembly, lead students and staff in repeating your motto. (Optional: Each team creates its own motto.)

Photographic Memories

In addition to or instead of the "Winners Photo Booth" suggested on page 25 for the Preview Event, provide other photo opportunities at the Preview Event, the Closing Ceremony closing program or other special events. Other photo opportunities could include the following:

⚽ Students stand with local athletes or a cardboard cutout of an athlete.

⚽ Students pose as if breaking the ribbon at the end of a race. A backdrop of a spectator-filled sports stadium would provide additional setting.

⚽ Provide one or more cardboard cutouts of athletes in action, but cut out the athletes' faces. Students put their faces into the openings and have their pictures taken.

Use the photos as a way to follow up unchurched families. After VBS, hand deliver the photos. Along with the photo, provide the families with a brochure of information about your church. In the brochure include Sunday School and worship service times, as well as a description of different ministry groups and contact information.

Official Name Tags

To make your staff and students look like official SonGames participants, use name tags that look like event tickets and attach them to Name Tag Ticket Holders (both items available from Gospel Light). Staff and students wear name tags around their necks.

Team Signs

Before VBS, have your teachers make cheer signs for their classes to hold up during assemblies: "Yea!" "We Love Our Team!" "Rah, Rah, Rah," etc. Or, have classes make signs on the first day in the Theme or Craft Center.

Parade of Teams

Like the Olympic parade of athletes, every day each class (team) parades around the Assembly Hall before taking their seats at both the Opening and Closing Assemblies. Teams may carry the signs suggested above, team flags created in Session 1 SonGames Training Center activity, Motto Pennants mounted on dowels or other SonGames or sports-related signs, flags or pennants.

Parlez en Français

French and English are the official languages of the Olympic Games and are used to announce all events, winners and medals. Sound officially Olympic by greeting students during each Opening Assembly by saying **Bonjour, étudiants. Bienvenue à SonGames!** (BAHN-jhuhr ay-TOO-dee-ahns. Bee-EHN-veh-noo ah

SonGames!) **Hello, students. Welcome to Son-Games!** Send them home from each Closing Assembly with *Au revoir. Voyez-vous la fois prochaine chez SonGames!* (auh reh-VWAH. Voy-YEH-voo lah fwah proh-CHAYN chay SonGames!) **Good bye. See you next time at SonGames!**

Bulletin Countdown
In your church bulletin and/or in the lobby of your church or other public area, provide a countdown for the 10 weeks prior to your VBS: "Only 72 more days till SonGames begins!" Each week update the countdown.

Daily News
Each day, create *Official SonGames 2004 Staff Update*—a daily newsletter just for your VBS staff. Print important announcements, contact names and numbers, revised schedules or other changes, as well as anecdotes and/or photos from the previous day's activities. Be sure to include the session motto and Bible memory verse. Pass the update out at morning staff devotional time or place them in the staff break area.

Flag Ceremony
Make a flag by painting the SonGames logo onto a length of fabric and attach it to a long pole. At each session's Opening Assembly, play "SonGames 2004 Fanfare" from *SonGames* cassette/CD as a volunteer carries in the flag and places it in a Christmas-tree or other stand. At the Closing Ceremony closing program, play the fanfare again as a volunteer carries the flag out of the assembly hall.

The Golden Shoe
Wash, dry and then spray-paint one or more discarded tennis shoes gold. Purchase shoes at a thrift store or ask congregation members to donate. Use the gold shoe(s) in one or more of the following ways:

⚽ **Offering** If you collect an offering at your VBS, consider passing around one or more golden shoes to collect it.

⚽ **Crafts** Paint one shoe for each student. Copy the memory verses or session motto onto 4-inch (10-cm) paper squares. Glue papers to craft sticks. Fill each shoe with plaster of paris. Plant verse, sports mottoes and/or artificial flowers in the shoe. Set aside to dry.

⚽ **Game** Plan a scavenger hunt to find the golden shoe.

⚽ **Award** In addition to or instead of distributing medals at each session's Closing Assembly, award the golden shoe (see p. 10).

Curriculum Resources
Familiarize yourself with the theme-related ideas provided throughout the curriculum. There may be ways to expand or adapt the ideas for use in other areas of your VBS. For instance, the team flags made during the first session of the SonGames Training Center have been suggested for use during the "Parade of Teams" on the previous page. Also, you could set aside time during your Session 2 Closing Assembly for students to trade the pins they made in the SonGames Training Center.

Panel of Experts
Visit the bulletin boards at the Gospel Light website, www.gospellight.com, for even more ideas provided by VBS directors throughout the United States and Canada.

Olympic Trivia
Use the following trivia facts each day at your opening or closing assembly or at any time you feel is appropriate.

⚽ Soccer, known as football in most of the world, has been played at all of the Olympic Games except the 1932 Games in Los Angeles, California. Women's soccer teams began competing at the Olympics in the 1996 Games in Atlanta, Georgia.

⚽ Track and field is called athletics in the Olympic Games, and it is the original Olympic sport. The very first event held in the ancient Olympic Games was a running sprint. They also had a race where the runners wore armor. Imagine running in a metal suit!

⚽ At the first modern Olympic Games in Athens, Greece, in 1896, the 1,200-meter freestyle swimming event was held in the Mediterranean Sea. A boat dropped the swimmers off in the icy water and they had to swim to shore! The winner was Hungarian swimmer Alfred Hajos, who said, "My will to live completely overcame my desire to win."

⚽ Though considered a single event, the decathlon is actually made up of ten different events: 100-meter dash, long jump, shot put, high jump, 400-meter dash, 110-meter hurdles, discus throw, pole vault, javelin throw, 1,500-meter run. Only men compete in the decathlon. Women compete in the heptathlon, which is made up of seven events: 100-meter hurdles, high jump, shot put, 200-meter dash, long jump, javelin throw, 800-meter run.

⚽ The Paralympic Games are for athletes with disabilities; but the sporting events are about the participants' athletic abilities, not their disabilities. Over the years, the games have grown tremendously in popularity. The first Paralympic Games were held in Rome, Italy, in 1960 and featured 400 athletes. At the 2000 Games in Sydney, Australia, there were 3,843 athletes from 122 countries.

Snapshot

Materials Preview

Starter Kit

Your Starter Kit contains samples of materials that have been carefully designed to help you promote and conduct an effective SonGames VBS. Each Starter Kit includes the following:

⚽ *Director's Guidebook*

⚽ *Preview Video* This video will give you a quick overview of SonGames that you can use to introduce your VBS to your staff, congregation, etc. Also included in this video are decorating ideas, suggested motions for the SonGames songs, recruiting commercials and testimonies of Olympic athletes, which can be shown to families as part of your closing program.

⚽ *Teacher Books* Teaching manuals for each age level contain what every teacher needs to lead stories, activities and games.

⚽ *Gold-Medal Crafts for Kids* craft book This book contains 45 great craft ideas using readily available materials, and reproducible coloring pages and certificates. Each *Teacher Book* refers to a specific project in the craft book for every lesson.

⚽ *Souvenir Guides* These colorful books for students are filled with Bible story reviews and fun life-application activities. Available for prekindergartners, kindergartners, primary children, middlers and preteens.

Souvenir Guide

⚽ *Director's Sample Pack* See description beginning on this page.

Director's Sample Pack

This pack includes a sample of each of the following:

⚽ **Clip Art Sheet** To build excitement about your upcoming VBS, use this clip art for your newsletters, bulletins and promotional materials. An attractive reproducible ad for use in your local newspaper or church newsletter is included. (Clip art is also available at www.gospellight.com and www.myvbs.com and on the *Clip Art & Publicity CD*.)

⚽ *God Cares for Me* **coloring book** This read-aloud story introduces children to the story of Paul's shipwreck on his way to Rome. The story is told in simple rhyming verses and has fun pictures to color. This is a great gift for VBS kids!

⚽ **Evangelism and Discipling Booklets** *God Loves You!* and *Growing as God's Child* will help you talk with students about becoming members of God's family and learning to live as His children.

⚽ **Helper Handbook** This handy booklet helps train VBS staff and contains daily devotionals, the Bible story, information to keep each staff member "on track" with each day's lesson and has a place for staff to record the essential information that they need.

⚽ **SonGames Songbook** These songs make Scripture truths come alive for singers and listeners alike. The book contains songs and motions for all ages.

⚽ **Peel 'n Press Stickers** These colorful stickers are perfect for awards and for charting students' progress and attendance.

⚽ **Wristband** These wristbands for students to wear come in six different colors. Use them to designate different teams. Use a permanent marker to write emergency phone numbers and names on wristbands for easy reference.

⚽ **Coloring Poster** Invite children to VBS by using this fun-to-color reproducible poster—distribute in Sunday School, at children's church, through the mail or in your neighborhood.

⚽ **Doorknob Hanger** Hang these colorful invitations to SonGames on the doors of neighborhood houses near your church.

⚽ **Name Tag** Names are important! Use these VBS name tags for each leader, teacher, student and visitor.

⚽ **Plastic Tote Bag** Give each child a perfect place to keep VBS papers and projects together. Provide each teacher a convenient way to store lesson materials.

⚽ **Bulletin Cover/Insert or Promotional Flyer** These full-color 8 1/2x11-inch (21.5x28-cm) sheets may be printed with your information on the back. Fold in half to use as bulletin covers, or cut apart to use as bulletin inserts or promotional flyers.

⚽ **Student Certificate** These colorful certificates can be given

to students for attendance and achievement.
- **Volunteer Certificate** Recognize and thank your teachers, leaders and helpers with this certificate.
- **Iron-On T-Shirt Transfer** Use this colorful design to identify staff or to give every child a personal SonGames memento.
- **Bookmark** Give away bookmarks as awards and prizes.
- **Invitation Postcard** Mail these full-color postcards to prospective students. Instant e-postcards are also available at www.myvbs.com.
- **Attendance/Memory Verse Chart** This colorful chart coordinates with theme stickers. Use it to record students' attendance or Bible Memory Verse memorization.
- **Theme Poster** Advertise your VBS in your community with this beautiful large poster. This poster is also available in a smaller size.

Super Decorating & Resource Pack

This pack includes essential resources for the classroom teacher as well as exciting decorating helps.
- **Teaching and Decorating Resources** There are two colorful resource books filled with ideas and materials to enhance Bible learning. The *Prekindergarten/Kindergarten Teaching and Decorating Resources* book contains Bible story visual aids, decorating patterns, Bible memory verse posters and other materials to use in activities. The *Elementary Teaching and Decorating Resources* book contains Bible memory verse posters, Bible story visual aids, patterns and other materials for activities.
- **SonGames T-Shirt** This adult-sized shirt is perfect attire for the VBS Director. Additional shirts may be purchased for each member of your staff.
- **Evangelism and Discipling Booklets** See description under Director's Sample Pack.
- **Motto Pennants** Use these colorful signs to designate classrooms, identify groups and review each session's motto.
- **Clip Art & Publicity CD** To build excitement about your upcoming VBS, use this clip art for your newsletters, bulletins and promotional materials. There are color as well as black and white images.

Music & Skit Production Pack

In this pack you'll find everything you need to lead music, stage skits and present the Closing Ceremony closing program.
- **SonGames CD** This reproducible CD contains a split-track recording for performance of all the songs. Additional early childhood songs, sound effects for skits and promotional radio spots are also included.
- **SonGames cassette** Make copies of this reproducible cassette for all your classroom teachers. This cassette contains the SonGames songs for all ages as well as additional early childhood songs. Use this cassette to make copies of the music for your students to take home or purchase the *Student Music Packs* described below.
- **SonGames Songbook** See description under Starter Kit.
- **Assemblies and Skits Production Guide** This reproducible book includes opening and closing assembly instructions, daily skit scripts and the Closing Ceremony skit script. Also included are patterns and directions for making the SonGames Backdrop and other props and set pieces. Use them to set the stage for your opening and closing assemblies as well as the Closing Ceremony closing program.
- **Teaming Up at SonGames Skit Video** Use this videocassette as a rehearsal help for your live skits or during your VBS in place of live skit presentations.

- **Student Music Packs** (not included in Music & Skit Production Pack) Instead of duplicating the SonGames music for all your VBS students, you may purchase these packs of 10 cassettes or 10 CDs. These cassettes and CDs contain all the SonGames music your students will love.

Super Starter Pack

This pack provides all you'll need for the best VBS ever. The Super Starter Pack includes all of the items previously described:
- **Starter Kit** (including Director's Sample Pack)
- **Super Decorating & Resource Pack**
- **Music & Skit Production Pack**

In addition, with your purchase of the Super Starter Pack, you will receive a CD to set up your own customizable website through www.myvbs.com. In addition to providing your church with an instant VBS website, www.myvbs.com provides you with SonGames clip art, an easy-to-use calendar, a budget calculator and additional helps for recruitment, training and publicizing your VBS. Visit www.myvbs.com to find out more.

Director's Planning Guide

1. Plan Your VBS Program

Summertime offers your church ideal opportunities for discipleship ministry and evangelistic outreach. Gospel Light's SonGames is an effective and appealing VBS program that can help you reach students and families in your church and community. Every element of the course has been written with spiritual growth and teaching flexibility in mind. SonGames can be used in a variety of formats.

Choose Your Format

Traditional 5-Day VBS

A 5-day VBS program is still the most common choice for VBS. A morning or afternoon time slot works very well if your families have a stay-at-home parent. However, an evening VBS makes staff recruitment easier and avoids day-care conflicts. But be aware that an evening program will often need to be shorter and may limit the number of activities you can include in each session.

10-Day VBS

While the 5-day VBS program is easier to staff and operate, the 10-day VBS plan may allow both learners and teachers to explore more thoroughly the Bible stories, memory verses and life lessons. You can easily expand SonGames into 10 days by using more of the activity centers and telling the Bible story one day and using the Bible Story Review Center to review the same Bible story the following day.

Intergenerational VBS

This unique approach brings entire families together for parts—or even all—of the VBS activities. Instead of dropping their children off for VBS, parents stay and participate in activities specially designed to strengthen family relationships (see appendix A, pp. 71-74).

Backyard Bible School

This format provides opportunities for neighborhood evangelism. Many children who do not attend church may feel more comfortable in the familiar surroundings of a neighbor's backyard than at a church (see appendix B, pp. 75-76).

Camps and Retreats

You can use your VBS in a day camp, residential camp or weekend retreat format. For day camps, extend your VBS day by arranging field trips and having children bring sack lunches. For camps or retreats, adapt your VBS materials as needed for an outdoor camp.

Opening and Closing Assemblies

Whichever format you choose, opening and closing assembly times can certainly generate excitement and enthusiasm within your VBS. See the *Assemblies and Skits Production Guide* for help in planning your assemblies. Choose an enthusiastic leader and coordinate with other staff who may be involved in the activities. Your assembly time may include
- Welcome, prayer and announcements
- SonGames songs
- Live or videotaped SonGames skits from *Assemblies and Skits Production Guide* and/or *Teaming Up at SonGames Skit Video*.
- Missions project updates

Choose Your Learning Plan

Once you've chosen your format, choose your learning plan. There are four learning plans from which to choose. Each plan impacts the tasks assigned to your staff and the daily schedule.

Activity Center Plan

Individual activities are set up in specific locations. Outdoor areas, classrooms or large multipurpose rooms may be used for activity centers. Children travel in age-level groups, rotating from center to center throughout the day, escorted by Guides, who may be adult leaders or youth helpers. Each center has one or two activity leaders who prepare and present only that specific activity as groups rotate through. This plan simplifies preparation for volunteers and allows them to work in their areas of strength, thus making recruiting easier (see "Activity Center Guide" on pp. 31-34).

Classroom-Based Plan

The teacher for each class teaches each day's Bible lesson and leads most or all of the other activities within a designated room. This plan allows each classroom to be set up for a specific age group. This approach is recommended for early childhood classes, regardless of the plan chosen for older children.

Modified Activity Center Plan

Many churches prefer a modified approach that assigns one or more teachers to each class for Bible teaching and life application but rotates children through centers for all other activities. This plan allows Bible teachers to get to know their children, plus provides children the variety of traveling to other locations for activities such as music and crafts.

Site-Based Plan

In this plan, every day a teacher teaches the same entire lesson at the same location to a new class. For example, the first-grade class stays in one room and completes Session 5 activities on the first day of VBS. On the second day of VBS, the class moves to another room for Session 1 with a different teacher. The main advantage is that teachers only need to prepare one lesson. Also, each room may be decorated for a particular Bible story.

There are a several disadvantages with a site-based plan: First, activities that involve all the children, such as assemblies, cannot reinforce the Bible lesson for that day because each class has a different Bible lesson. Second, the lessons cannot progress chronologically or toward a climax because each class will be using a different lesson as the VBS concludes.

Planning Your Early Childhood VBS

Course Overview

The Bible stories, Bible verses and lesson focus statements used in the elementary curriculums have been modified to present concepts to young children at an age-appropriate level. (See chart at bottom of page.)

The Early Childhood Classroom

Young children have very specific physical and cognitive needs that differ significantly from those of school-aged children. We can best help preschoolers learn Bible truths by providing active play experiences that a teacher connects to Bible stories and verses through comments and questions.

This is why we recommend a classroom-based plan for early childhood classrooms, no matter which plan is used for elementary classes (see top of this page). In the classroom-based plan, children spend the entire session in the same classroom with the same teachers. (Note: Separate craft and/or recreation leaders may lead these activities.) In addition to providing adequate time for learning, the self-contained classroom provides the sense of familiarity and security needed by young children.

Part of creating an environment conducive to learning for young children is to have familiar items in the classroom. On the next page we describe ways to decorate your early childhood classroom in theme-specific ways. In addition, your children will benefit from having familiar classroom materials available to them. Some suggested items:

⚽ **Blocks** Wooden, plastic or cardboard blocks in different sizes, shapes and colors; toy people

Course Overview for Early Childhood Classroom

Session	Bible Story	Scripture	Bible Words	Lesson Focus
1	Jesus Loves Paul	Acts 9:1-22	"God made us and we are his." (See Psalm 100:3.)	God sent Jesus to show His love for me.
2	Friends Help Paul	Acts 9:19-25	"Help each other show love." (See Hebrews 10:24.)	God gives me friends so that we can help each other.
3	Paul's in Jail!	Acts 16:16-35	"I am quick to obey God's Word." (See Psalm 119:32.)	God helps me to obey His Word and do good.
4	Paul's Stormy Trip	Acts 27	"Do not fear, for I am with you." Isaiah 41:10	God promises to be with me when I am afraid.
5	Paul Is Thankful	Acts 28	"Thanks be to God!" 1 Corinthians 15:57	God always loves me and helps me.

and animals; toy vehicles; manipulative building toys (Legos, Lincoln Logs, etc.).

⚽ **Art** Crayons, markers and chalk; a variety of paper (construction, white, butcher, etc.); play dough and dough toys; child-sized scissors.

⚽ **Dramatic Play** Dolls (with rubber molded heads), doll clothes and bedding; home-living furniture (kitchen appliances, rocking chairs, doll beds, etc.) and accessories (dishes, toy food, dress-up clothes for both boys and girls, etc.)

⚽ **Books** Variety of picture books

Many churches find it helpful to recruit an Early Childhood Director (see p. 15) who oversees and trains early childhood teachers.

Decorating the Early Childhood Classroom

Each day children will participate in one to four Bible Learning Activity centers in their classrooms. With a few decorations, each center can become a special place to visit at SonGames. If you do not wish to set up all the centers, use or adapt any of the ideas to decorate your classroom. *Prekindergarten/Kindergarten Teaching and Decorating Resources* contains all the instructions and patterns you'll need for decorating. (Tip: Ask people who cannot otherwise help at VBS to assist in designing and decorating rooms the weekend before VBS begins.)

Schedule for Each Session

BEFORE CLASS

Teacher's Devotional
Every teacher should prayerfully read each session's devotional to prepare his or her mind and heart for this ministry.

Staff Prayer
Set aside a place where staff may come to pray before each session. Pray specifically for children and staff who have special needs. Allow a few moments for special announcements or last-minute organizational details.

CLASS TIME

Adjust the length of each time segment to best fit the needs of your VBS.

Bible Learning Activity Centers
(40-45 minutes)

Welcome Time At the door, a designated teacher welcomes and assists each child in choosing an activity center.

Tumbelina's Gym (Movement and Games)

Sports-R-Fun Store (Dramatic Play)

Together Time, Bible Story and Music Fun/Good-Byes

Celebration Square (Art)

Super Sports Park (Blocks)

Activities Each teacher leads activity and conversation related to the Lesson Focus in one or more activity centers. Children are free to move from one center to another. Older children may rotate from activity to activity in groups. Don't worry if children don't want to participate in the suggested activity and create their own playtime activity. Teachers will still find the suggested conversation for each activity a helpful guide in talking about the day's focus.

Cleanup Time Teachers lead children in putting away materials.

Together Time
(10-15 minutes)
Teachers and children gather in one group for music, prayer, finger fun, a puppet activity and Bible Words.

Bible Story/Application
(15-20 minutes)
Children go to Bible story groups (about six children per teacher) or gather with entire class as one teacher presents Bible story using visual aids from the resource book. Then teacher and helpers sit at tables with children and guide them in completing Bible story and application activity pages from either the prekindergarten or kindergarten *Souvenir Guides*.

Recreation Game/Snack
(20-35 minutes)
Teachers (or a recreation leader) guide children in outdoor play activities, toileting and washup before snack. Check registration cards for any food allergies children may have. Also post a note each day alerting parents to the snack you will serve each day. Teachers sit with children during snack and help as needed.

Skit
(10-15 minutes)
Each day for elementary children, a humorous skit is usually presented during the Opening Assembly or at another time. If prekindergarten and kindergarten children aren't included in the Opening Assembly, have skit characters visit your classroom to talk with children, or simply show a portion of the *Teaming Up at SonGames Skit Video*.

Craft
(15-20 minutes)
Children return to class groups or go to craft center to complete a project from *Gold-Medal Crafts for Kids* craft book.

Music Fun/Good-Byes
(10-15 minutes)
Children gather for music, puppet time and indoor game activities until parents arrive. Children may place stickers on Sports Kids cutouts for saying the Bible verse of the day.

Training for Early Childhood Teachers and Helpers

Schedule a planning meeting for teachers and helpers several weeks before VBS. This meeting would take place at the same time as the planning meetings for other age-levels (see "Train Your VBS Staff," p. 19).

Before Your Planning Meeting
1. Carefully read the information provided in the *Prekindergarten/Kindergarten Teacher Book*. Note learning aims, Bible Learning Activity centers and schedule.
2. Give each teacher and helper the resources listed in "Staffing Needs" (see p. 14).
3. Make the following assignments for this meeting:

⚽ Ask each teacher to read "Age-Level Characteristics" (*Teacher Book,* p. 48) and "Storytelling Tips" (*Teacher Book,* p. 6).

⚽ Ask one teacher to prepare the Session 1 Bible story using visuals from *Prekindergarten/Kindergarten Teaching and Decorating Resources*.

⚽ Ask another teacher to describe *Souvenir Guide* Session 1 activities and tell how they help accomplish Bible learning aims.

⚽ Ask a teacher to make a sample of the Session 1 project from the *Gold-Medal Crafts for Kids* craft book and explain how to complete the craft.

⚽ Ask a teacher to become familiar with using the puppet, songs and finger fun suggested for each day. (See the *SonGames Songbook* for songs.)

4. Gather supplies and equipment for the course.

At the Planning Meeting
1. Begin on time. Pray together, asking God to help you express His love to children in ways they can understand.
2. Briefly review the following items, answering questions as needed for your VBS:

⚽ Session learning aims;

⚽ Schedule (beginning on p. 12);

⚽ The responsibilities of each teacher and helper. Decide which Bible Learning Activity centers to offer each day, with each teacher selecting an activity to lead. Make special assignments such as greeting children, recreation responsibilities and snack preparation.

3. Walk through Session 1 by having teachers share prepared assignments.
4. Present information related to Closing Program and additional ideas for reaching unchurched families (*Teacher Book,* p. 47).

2. Recruit Your VBS Staff

Guidelines for Successful Staff Recruitment

Recruiting personnel is one of your most important duties as Director. You can build a strong VBS staff by keeping the following guidelines in mind:

⚽ Start early (see "Director's Countdown Calendar" on p. 22).

⚽ Pray for guidance in finding the right people to serve in this ministry.

⚽ Write a clear job description for each position to be filled (see "Staffing Needs" beginning on this page).

⚽ Build a list of prospective staff members including former VBS workers, youth, parents, college students and senior citizens.

⚽ Share further recruiting responsibilities with the VBS leaders you recruit first.

⚽ Regularly present information to the congregation about your VBS program and volunteer opportunities. Show a segment of the *Preview Video* in a church service. Distribute volunteer recruitment flyers in your church bulletin or in personal mailings.

⚽ Personally contact each prospect. Challenge each one with the importance of this ministry. Explain the training and resources you will offer to help the prospect succeed. If you must recruit a large number of people, schedule meetings with groups of prospects.

⚽ Allow the prospect time to pray about the opportunity. Resist the temptation to arm-twist; you don't want to end up with reluctant personnel.

⚽ Screen all potential staff. Use your church's forms and policies to select responsible volunteers.

Staffing Needs

The following list of jobs includes a brief job description. Following each description is a list of suggested resources for each person in that position.

All VBS Plans

Director

Plans VBS format and schedule, recruits and trains staff and determines room assignments; oversees daily VBS activities.

⚽ *Director's Guidebook*

⚽ *Director's Sample Pack*

(Note: Both resources are included in both the Starter Kit and the Super Starter Pack.)

Helpers

Assist teachers and activity leaders with their responsibilities. These helpers can be adults or youth helpers (see "Using Youth Helpers" on p. 17).

⚽ *Helper Handbook*

Secretary/Registrar

Registers children, maintains records and prepares visitor information for follow-up.

Publicity Coordinator

Plans and carries out publicity to both church and community.

⚽ "Publicity Guide" from *Director's Guidebook* (pp. 27-30)

Special Events Coordinator

Plans and recruits staff for closing program, field trips, promotional events and other special events.

⚽ "Special Events" from *Director's Guidebook* (pp. 23-26)

⚽ *Helper Handbook*

Assembly Leader

Leads large group assemblies (Opening Assembly, Closing Assembly, Closing Ceremony closing program). This job is often performed by the VBS Director or Skit Leader.

⚽ *Assemblies and Skits Production Guide*

⚽ *Helper Handbook*

Additional Staff Helpful for Directors of Larger Programs

Assistant Director
Helps director with all responsibilities (in many churches, this person will be next year's Director). Maintains daily time schedule.
- *Director's Guidebook*

Decorating Coordinator
Plans and supervises decorating; recruits volunteers to help with decorating as needed.

- "Decorating Ideas" from *Preview Video*
- "Decorating Ideas" and patterns from *Teaching and Decorating Resources* books

Early Childhood Director
Supervises departmental activities and helps recruit and train teachers and helpers.
- "Planning Your Early Childhood VBS" from *Director's Guidebook* (pp. 11-13)
- *Prekindergarten/Kindergarten Teacher Book*

Department Leaders
Supervise departmental activities and help recruit age-level staff.
- *Teacher Book* for the appropriate age level

Follow-Up Coordinator
Prepares and distributes correspondence from the appropriate church contact people to unchurched VBS attendees. This role would be a natural fit for someone from your church's outreach/evangelism committee who understands children's ministry.
- "Evangelism" section from *Director's Guidebook* (p. 21)
- "Follow-Up" section from *Director's Guidebook* (p. 21)
- *Helper Handbook*

Prayer Leader
Recruits people to pray for the teachers, volunteers, students and families participating in your VBS.
- *Helper Handbook*

Finance Coordinator
Plans budget and sees that money allocated for the program is spent appropriately.

Missions and Service Coordinator
Plans and supervises the missions project or other service projects, and leads or recruits a leader for the Missions and Service Center (if needed).
- "Missions and Service Center" from *Director's Guidebook* (pp. 53-60)
- *Helper Handbook*

Skit Leader
Auditions and/or recruits actors; schedules and directs rehearsals; supervises preparation of the backdrop and props.
- *Assemblies and Skits Production Guide*
- *Teaming Up at SonGames Skit Video*
- *Helper Handbook*

Youth Coordinator
Enlists, trains and supervises middle school and high school youth serving as helpers in VBS.
- "Using Youth Helpers" from *Director's Guidebook* (p. 17)
- *Helper Handbook*

Activity Center Plan

Recruit leaders for each of the activity centers you have chosen for your VBS.

(Note: We recommend the classroom-based model for early childhood classes. See "Classroom-Based and Early Childhood Plan" on p. 16 for the resources needed by these teachers.)

Guides
Essential to the Activity Center Plan are the Guides. Each adult Guide escorts a group of students to the different activity centers. Because they spend the entire session with one group of students, they are able to build relationships with children, assist children in various activities and maintain discipline. Guides should be prepared to talk and pray with children about becoming members of God's family.
- *Helper Handbook*
- *God Loves You!* and *Growing as God's Child* booklets.

Elementary Bible Story Leader
Teaches the Bible story and leads the life-application time as each group of students visits the Bible Story/Life Application Center. (Note: Some churches combine the positions of Guide and Bible Story Leader.)
- *Teacher Book* for each age level
- *Elementary Teaching and Decorating Resources*
- *Souvenir Guides*, one for each student

Craft Leader

Chooses craft projects, gathers materials, explains and supervises the crafts as each group of students visits the Craft Center; may recruit helpers.

⚽ *Gold-Medal Crafts for Kids* craft book

⚽ *Helper Handbook*

Recreation Game Leader

Chooses games, gathers supplies and leads children in playing the games; may recruit helpers.

⚽ "Recreation Game Center" from *Director's Guidebook* (pp. 61-64)

⚽ *Helper Handbook*

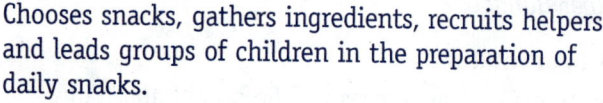

Snack Leader

Chooses snacks, gathers ingredients, recruits helpers and leads groups of children in the preparation of daily snacks.

⚽ "Snack Center" from *Director's Guidebook* (pp. 65-70)

⚽ *Helper Handbook*

Missions and Service Leader

Educates students and staff about chosen missions or service project; directs all missions or service project activities; collects and distributes donated money or other items.

⚽ "Missions and Service Center" from *Director's Guidebook* (pp. 53-60)

⚽ *Helper Handbook*

Music Leader

Directs activities in the Music Center and leads or assists in leading singing during assemblies. Prepares children to present music during the closing program.

⚽ *SonGames Songbook*

⚽ *SonGames* cassette or CD

⚽ "Song Motions" from *Preview Video*

⚽ *Helper Handbook*

⚽ Optional: *Student Music Packs* cassettes or CDs

Bible Memory Verse Leader

Plans, gathers materials and leads games as each group of students visits the Bible Memory Verse Center. Uses suggested conversation to link the Bible verse and students' activities to their everyday lives.

⚽ *Teacher Books* for appropriate ages, or "Bible Memory Verse Center" from *Director's Guidebook* (p. 41)

⚽ Memory Verse Posters from *Elementary Teaching and Decorating Resources*

⚽ *Helper Handbook*

Bible Story Review Leader

Plans, gathers materials and leads games as each group of students visits the Bible Story Review Center. Uses suggested conversation to help children review each day's Bible story and apply it to their lives.

⚽ *Teacher Books* for appropriate ages, or "Bible Story Review Center" from *Director's Guidebook* (pp. 47-52)

⚽ *Helper Handbook*

SonGames Training Center Leader

Plans, gathers the materials and leads activities as each group of students visits the SonGames Training Center. Uses suggested conversation to link students' activities to their everyday lives.

⚽ *Teacher Books* for appropriate ages, or "SonGames Training Center" from *Director's Guidebook* (pp. 35-40)

⚽ Sports Motto Posters and Decathlon Cards from *Elementary Teaching and Decorating Resources*

⚽ *Helper Handbook*

Classroom-Based and Early Childhood Plan

Age-Level Teachers

Plan and present the entire lesson (Bible story, games, music, crafts, etc.) to a class in one classroom.

For Each Teacher:

⚽ *Teacher Book* for appropriate age level

⚽ *Souvenir Guides* for appropriate age level, one for each student

⚽ *Teaching and Decorating Resources* for appropriate age level

⚽ *Gold-Medal Crafts for Kids* craft book

If teacher is also teaching music, he or she will need

⚽ *SonGames Songbook*

⚽ *SonGames* cassette or CD

⚽ "Song Motions" from *Preview Video*

Using Youth Helpers

Many churches find great value in using middle school and high school young people in leadership roles in Vacation Bible School. It's good for the children—they readily admire and enjoy following a young person's guidance and look forward to becoming helpers themselves. It's good for the adult staff—they benefit from the energy and enthusiasm of young assistants. And it's good for the young people—they gain valuable ministry experience and personal spiritual growth.

The following guidelines have proven helpful:

1. Far in advance of VBS, **talk with the church's youth leaders** about involving young people. Enlist their support in encouraging youth participation. Seek to involve at least some of the youth leaders in various phases of VBS and its preparation.

2. Recruit a **Youth Coordinator** (see description on p. 15).

3. Define **requirements** for the young people. Within the framework of your church's youth programs and child-safety policies, set standards that will challenge young people while being as inclusive as possible. Often young people will blossom when given the opportunity to serve.

4. Decide on the **positions** young people can fill. The specific tasks may vary depending on how you structure your VBS.

   All VBS Plans:
   Skit performers, musicians, Bible verse listeners, and other positions specific to your VBS.

   Activity Center Plan:
   ⚽ Youth helpers assist adult guides and stay with the same group of children as they move from activity to activity, focusing on building friendships and keeping children involved. It is a good idea to have both a boy and a girl with each group of children, providing role models for both genders.
   ⚽ Youth helpers stay in an assigned activity area (Bible story, crafts, games, snack, etc.), assisting the leader(s) with specific functions.

   Classroom-Based and Early Childhood Plan:
   ⚽ Youth helpers assist leaders and stay in the same room with the same children and staff for most activities, performing a combination of tasks.

5. Enlist young people to serve. At least several months in advance of VBS, begin announcing this opportunity to youths and their parents. Provide recruiting flyers to interested youths (p. 18). Promote the benefit of including youth helpers to your congregation and VBS families. Present it as a great opportunity for children to benefit from positive youth role models.

6. Working with your Youth Coordinator, prayerfully assign specific positions to your youth helpers.

7. Schedule one or more training sessions in advance of VBS just for the youth helpers. Make the sessions very specific in covering what you expect of them. Provide each volunteer with a copy of the *Helper Handbook* and go over its material during your training session(s). It is important that youth helpers be familiar with each day's focus, Bible memory verse and Bible story. Challenge them to make this event more than just a fun time playing with the children.

8. Prepare your adult staff to work with the youth helpers. Provide the adults with information explaining the youth helpers' responsibilities. Encourage adults not to limit young people to busy work, but to also assign jobs the young person will view as meaningful.

9. Schedule at least one meeting with all staff together to help adults and youth get to know each other and to finalize plans and assignments for each person.

10. During VBS, plan for ways to make sure youth helpers have a good time and feel appreciated. Ideas to accomplish this:

    ⚽ Provide a special treat each day.

    ⚽ Encourage the children to thank their youth helpers. (Affirmation from children is one of the biggest benefits helpers will receive.)

    ⚽ During each opening or closing assembly, comment on the great job the youth are doing.

    ⚽ Have a youth leader, one who already knows the youth, make a point of checking in with each young person, affirming their work and seeing if there are any problems or difficulties.

    ⚽ Schedule a special event just for the youth helpers, such as a pizza party, a picnic in the afternoon, a social event in the evening, etc.

Sample Flyers for Staff Recruitment

Vacation Bible School Volunteers

Dates _____

Time _____

I would like to help in one or more of the following areas (please circle):

- Decorating
- Prayer support
- Publicity
- Missions project
- Bible teaching
- Crafts
- Group Guide
- Recreation games
- Activity centers
- Music
- Skits
- Snacks
- Special events
- Follow-up

Name

_____

Address

_____

Phone (day)

_____

Phone (evening)

_____

E-mail

_____

If you have any questions about Vacation Bible School or your involvement in it, please call

_____
(name)

_____
(phone number)

PLEASE RETURN THIS FLYER IN THE OFFERING PLATE OR TO THE CHURCH OFFICE.

Vacation Bible School Volunteers

Dates _____ Time _____

Before VBS, I would like to help by (circle one or more):

- Praying for teachers and children
- Providing craft materials
- Preparing craft materials
- Planning decorations
- Decorating
- Gathering props for decorations and/or skits
- Planning publicity
- Distributing publicity materials
- Painting banners, backdrops, sets, etc.
- Preregistering children
- Planning special events (promotional day, field trips, etc.)
- Assisting with special events

During VBS, I would like to help in one or more of the following areas (please circle):

Bible Story/Life Application	Leader	Helper
Bible Memory Verse game	Leader	Helper
Bible Story Review game	Leader	Helper
SonGames Training Center activity	Leader	Helper
Craft	Leader	Helper
Recreation Game	Leader	Helper
Snack	Leader	Helper
Music	Leader	Helper
Missions	Leader	Helper
Special Events	Leader	Helper

- Secretary/Registrar
- Skit Director
- Actor
- Photographer/Videographer
- Assembly Leader
- Follow-Up
- Helper

Age Level Preference

Prekindergarten (3-4 yrs.)   Kindergarten (5 yrs.)

1st grade   2nd grade   3rd grade

4th grade   5th grade   6th grade

Name _____

Address _____

Phone (day) _____

Phone (evening) _____

E-mail _____

If you have any questions about Vacation Bible School or your involvement in it, please call

_____
(name and phone number)

PLEASE RETURN THIS FLYER TO THE CHURCH OFFICE.

3. Train Your VBS Staff

There are basically two types of training sessions that should be conducted: general (for all staff) and specific (departmental or leadership staff).

A **general meeting** for all volunteers is absolutely necessary for dispersing basic VBS information. One or two meetings are all that you will probably need to have. These meetings should include the following:

- Introduction to the curriculum (theme, lesson focus, theme verse, etc.)
- Pertinent general information (dates, time schedule, locations, supplies, future meetings, etc.)
- Opportunity to fellowship

Specific meetings should then be conducted by the director or by department leaders. The nature of these meetings depends on the needs of the staff. Topics that may be covered in these sessions:

- Planning and preparing lessons
- Decorating and preparing your classroom
- Use of the curriculum
- Age-level characteristics
- How to lead a child to Christ (see p. 33 in *Helper Handbook* or p. 1 in *Teacher Books*)
- Dealing with discipline
- Building relationships
- Storytelling techniques
- Following up after VBS

Preparing for the Meetings

- Schedule each meeting at a time you think most volunteers will be able to attend. Many churches schedule their meetings on Saturday morning or Sunday, after church. Provide child care if needed. Reserve your chosen dates on the church calendar.

- As you begin recruiting, make sure you let all volunteers know the dates of your meetings—either in person, by phone, by mail or by e-mail. Publicize each meeting in your church bulletin. Then mail reminder notices at least five days in advance. Make your notices look attractive and exciting, and be sure to include the date, time and place.

- Plan each meeting's agenda. Write down all the information and topics you wish to cover. Have specific goals, and plan specific steps to meet them. If other individuals will lead parts of the meeting, make sure you give them plenty of advance notice. Begin brainstorming ideas on how to add excitement and variety to your presentation. Consider using visuals, skits, games, videos, etc.

- Make a list of all the supplies you will need for each meeting. Secure important curriculum items such as the preview video, musical tape or CD, posters, teacher books and any other helpful promotional items. Also make sure you have tables, chairs, cassette or CD player, a television, VCR and overhead projector, if needed.

- Plan to serve refreshments. Refreshments show your volunteers you appreciate their attendance. The food can be as simple as coffee, iced tea and cookies or can be expanded to include theme-oriented munchies.

- Personalize each meeting. Purchase or make name tags for all your volunteers—don't assume everyone knows each other. Provide a sign-in sheet to give your volunteers a sense of accountability. Purchase little treats such as candy, VBS buttons or pins, note pads and/or tote bags for each participant.

Hints for Successful Meetings

- Arrive early. Having everything planned and set up in advance provides a positive example for your volunteers. You can't expect your volunteers to do more than you're willing to do yourself.

- Use your VBS theme to build excitement. Reinforce the theme through the use of music, decorations, attire, refreshments, prizes, etc.

- Provide some time for fellowship. Start each meeting with an icebreaker game or other fun event. This will help your volunteers become familiar with one another, build friendships and foster team unity.

- Make the meetings worth their while. Though "fun" can be on the agenda, volunteers should not feel that they have wasted their time. Make sure all information is clearly presented.

- Start and end meetings on time. This shows your volunteers that you respect their schedules. Allow about five minutes for volunteers to arrive before beginning the meeting.

4. Publicize Your VBS

Below is a list of ways to promote your VBS both within your church and in your community. For an explanation of how to use each item listed, a suggested publicity calendar and other helps, see "Publicity Guide" on pages 27-30 and "SonGames 2004 Preview Event" on pages 24-26.

Build VBS Interest Within the Church

- Bulletin Insert
- Preview Video
- VBS Video
- Posters
- Sunday School Visits
- Church Website
- Information Booth
- SonGames Skits
- VBS Buttons and T-Shirts
- Music

Reach Out to Children from the Community

- Outdoor Banner or Sign
- Posters
- Invitation Postcards
- Promotional Flyers and/or Doorknob Hangers
- SonGames Skits
- Radio
- Newspaper, Television and Other Media
- SonGames 2004 Preview Event
- Preregistration Bonuses
- Direct Mail
- Prizes
- Parents' Class

VBS Buttons

SonGames Registration, VBS 2004

Name _____

Street Address _____

City _____ State _____ Zip _____

Home Phone (_____) _____

Parent(s) name(s) _____

Parent(s) work phone(s) _____

In case of emergency, contact _____

Allergies or other medical conditions _____

School grade just completed _____

Name of home church, if any _____

5. Evangelism

The apostle Paul wrote, "I pray that you may be active in sharing your faith" (Philemon 1:6). SonGames presents a unique opportunity to share the gospel and win people to Christ.

⚽ Give staff members the Gospel Light booklets *God Loves You!* (for leading children to Christ) and *Growing as God's Child* (for follow-up and discipling).

⚽ Be sure staff members are familiar with the articles and lessons in the *Teacher Books* that focus on presenting the gospel (look for the evangelism opportunity symbol).

Teacher Book

⚽ Instruct leaders and teachers to invite responses by saying, "If you're interested in knowing about becoming a member of God's family, I'll be here after class to talk with you." Children sometimes feel hesitant to seek out busy adults, so encourage teachers to be ready to schedule a brief quiet time to talk informally with individual children.

6. Follow-Up

⚽ Before VBS begins, have the Follow-Up Coordinator prepare various notes to be mailed to each visiting student and family after VBS. Notes may be sent from the VBS teacher, the pastor and/or a potential Sunday School teacher. Names and addresses can be obtained from the Secretary/Registrar. Have teachers personalize and sign these notes during VBS. The Follow-Up Coordinator can mail them out separately in the week or two following VBS.

⚽ During VBS the Follow-Up Coordinator should give teachers a take-home note for each student, thanking the parents for sending the student, inviting families to attend the Closing Ceremony closing program, offering a visit from a church leader and suggesting any other family-oriented programs that your church provides. Have the teachers send the note home with each student.

⚽ Suggest that Sunday School teachers attend the Closing Ceremony closing program. Ask age-level teachers or guides to introduce visiting children and their parents to the appropriate Sunday School teachers.

⚽ At the Closing Ceremony closing program, set up a free family photo opportunity with simple costumes and a backdrop. After photographs are printed, personally deliver them to unchurched families along with a brochure describing your church's ministry programs.

⚽ If you present a video or slideshow of highlights from your VBS as part of your Closing Ceremony closing program, offer to give copies to families. As with the photo suggestion above, following VBS, volunteers make and distribute videocassettes or CDs along with a church-ministry brochure.

⚽ Present a participation certificate to each student and an appreciation certificate to each volunteer. Samples of full-color certificates are available in the Director's Sample Pack and can be ordered in bulk from Gospel Light. Reproducible certificates are printed in the *Gold-Medal Crafts for Kids* craft book.

⚽ Plan a children's or family activity in the month following VBS (see "Special Events," pp. 23-26). Distribute a flyer during VBS and mail a flyer to each new visitor a week or two prior to the event. Finally, give each visitor's family a friendly invitation by phone the week leading up to the event.

⚽ In the fall, when it is time to register children for the coming year's Sunday School classes, send an invitation to parents and children. Be sure to include service times, directions to the Sunday School classrooms, the name of the teacher of the child who had attended VBS and information about other classes for children and adults. Include the name and phone number of someone to be contacted for more information.

Director's Countdown Calendar

Personalize and adapt this calendar according to your own church's needs. Your support staff can execute many of the items on this list.

20 Weeks Before:
- Pray, asking for God's help and guidance as you plan and organize your VBS.
- Determine time, format, learning plan and location of VBS (Activity Center Plan, Backyard Bible School, camp, etc.).
- Set VBS dates in conjunction with all-church calendar.
- Order Starter Kit or Super Starter Pack.

18 Weeks Before:
- Recruit an assistant director and publicity coordinator.

16 Weeks Before:
- Meet with assistant director and publicity coordinator:
  1. Pray for VBS.
  2. Outline daily VBS time schedule.
  3. Set deadline dates for all preparations.
  4. List all staff needs.
  5. Compile lists of prospective workers.
  6. Plan training meetings.
- Order curriculum materials for all teachers, leaders and students (use last year's attendance reports as a guide).
- Plan and order publicity materials.
- Enclose a customized personnel recruitment flyer in the church bulletin or newsletter (see p. 18).

12 Weeks Before:
- Begin personal contacts (letters and/or phone calls) to recruit rest of staff. In larger churches recruit department leaders and a craft leader for each age group.

10 Weeks Before:
- Meet with leaders to plan training meetings and assign responsibilities.
- Contact all recruits, confirming preliminary assignments and notifying them of training meetings.
- Plan dedication service for workers; secure minister's approval and help.
- Meet with Special Events Coordinator and plan SonGames 2004 Preview Event and Closing Ceremony closing program.
- Plan follow-up efforts with evangelism and Sunday School leaders.
- Plan missions project.

8 Weeks Before:
- Announce training meetings. Identify any new staff additions and remaining vacancies.
- Make bulletin or newsletter insert listing craft supplies, refreshments and other materials needed.

4 Weeks Before:
- Distribute curriculum samples to teachers and other leaders.
- Conduct training meetings:
  1. Present overview of course content and show *Preview Video*.
  2. Sing SonGames songs.
  3. Explain time schedule and staff responsibilities.
  4. Have teachers and leaders meet together to prepare lesson and activity plans.
- Meet with the coordinators (missions, publicity, special events, finance, crafts, snacks, etc.) for prayer and to assess progress.
- Begin preregistration, assign children to classes, and prepare name tags.
- Check donations and purchase additional supplies as needed.
- Dedicate the VBS workers in church service.

During VBS:
- Pray with and for your staff regularly.
- Enthusiastically encourage workers with notes and visits to classes.
- Secure additional supplies as needed.
- Visit classes; make any necessary adjustments regarding staffing, transitions between activities, etc.
- Have someone available to run errands.
- Make sure attendance records are carefully kept and contact information is complete for each visiting student.
- Send home Invitation Postcards to invite parents to the Closing Ceremony closing program.

After VBS:
- Express appreciation to all workers with a note or a small gift.
- Mail follow-up postcards to VBS visitors to begin contact efforts.
- See that supplies are packed, labeled and stored for next year.
- Compile all records, including sample flyers, bulletin announcements, finance records and staff and student lists. Note how problems were solved and how to avoid similar problems. Include notes of necessary adjustments in schedules, additional supplies needed, etc.

Special Events

Imagine the impact on children's lives in your community if you expand SonGames outside your congregation or beyond five days! Extra days can give your children special opportunities to deepen relationships and apply what they are learning about being members of God's team. Add a day, a week or a summer of fun to your SonGames experience!

For even more ideas for expanding SonGames, read the service project ideas on pages 53-54.

Field Trips

⚽ **Sports Park** If you have a nearby sports park, plan a trip for staff and students. Water slides, batting cages, paddle boats, bowling, climbing walls and miniature golf are all fun activities to capture the interest of everyone involved.

⚽ **Sporting Event** Consider organizing a trip to a ballgame, gymnastics competition, swim meet or other sporting event. It doesn't matter if it's a major-league team or a local tournament!

⚽ **Local Park** Reserve space at a local park to stage your own sporting event. Grill hamburgers and hot dogs and provide other picnic favorites to eat. If you plan the event before VBS, pass out brochures or flyers about SonGames to interested passersby.

Events at Church

⚽ **Games on Film** Show a video of Olympic highlights or a movie about sports or athletes. (Consider *Chariots of Fire*. This film is about missionary Eric Liddle and his 1924 Olympic trials and triumphs.) Serve snacks made from recipes on pages 65-70 or other favorite recipes.

⚽ **Crafts Workshop** Choose one of the more challenging projects from *Gold-Medal Crafts for Kids* craft book and set aside a day or evening to make the project. Break up your time by gathering for a few minutes of singing VBS songs and a snack. Invite your pastor or another teacher to dress in sports clothing and read a children's storybook about sports or the Olympic Games.

⚽ **Tournament of Champions** If your church has sports facilities of any kind, consider a tournament between different adult Sunday School or other fellowship groups. Basketball, soccer, baseball and volleyball are all sports many churches have facilities to play.

⚽ **Mini-Olympics** For a weekend or evening event, set up a variety of outdoor physical activities and games. Divide group into teams with sports-related names.

⚽ **Sports Hero** Invite a local sports hero who is experienced in public speaking to come to your church for a special presentation and/or demonstration. Many retired professional and Olympic athletes specialize in conducting events of this type.

SonGames 2004 Preview Event

Special Events

Publicize your upcoming VBS by having a promotional event: SonGames 2004 Preview Event. This event is a great opportunity to reach out to children and families in your community and to build enthusiasm for VBS among the people of your church.

The Preview Event includes games, activities and snacks—all related to SonGames VBS. Admission is free. In this informal atmosphere, non-Christian parents will feel comfortable visiting your church with their children and will appreciate the good time you provide at no cost. And most important, children won't want to miss out on all the fun they will have at your VBS.

Your primary goal at the SonGames 2004 Preview Event is to motivate the parents and children who attend to enroll in your upcoming VBS program. Schedule your event one to three weeks before VBS. There are several things you can do to ensure that your promotion day leads to meaningful publicity for your VBS.

Staffing

⚽ Each activity needs at least one adult or youth helper to be in charge. Encourage adult and youth helpers to dress in sports clothing.

⚽ Ask individual families or adult Sunday School classes in your church to be "Official SonGames Sponsors" and organize a booth.

⚽ Have several helpers or the skit characters greet parents and encourage children to try an activity that is low on participation.

Registration and Information Booth

Set up a tent or table near the entrance to your SonGames 2004 Preview Event. At this site, parents may register their children for VBS.

Give each student a Preview Event Pass that will allow him or her to participate in all activities and refreshments, and a small gift such as a button to wear. When students participate in an activity, they get their passes punched or receive a sticker on the space marked on the pass for that activity.

Note: This pass can also be given out in advance at Sunday School, a park, a shopping center or door-to-door, etc., to promote SonGames.

Setup

Transform your church parking lot (and/or lawn) into a sports complex with games, activities and snacks. Designate each activity area with colored chalk; an awning, stakes and rope; or even booths. Tents and awnings can to be used for appropriate activities.

Sporty Snacks

Set up a refreshment center and serve any or all of the following snacks and drinks:

Sports Drinks Provide ice-cold water, juice and/or sports drinks to replenish body fluids.

Concessions Serve standard concession foods such as

⚽ **Ice Cream** Serve in a cone or a small paper cup.

⚽ **Corn Dogs** Serve corn dogs with ketchup or mustard.

⚽ **Soft Pretzels** Serve a soft pretzel with mustard or cheese dip.

Consider renting snow-cone, popcorn or cotton-candy machines from a party supply company.

International Snacks Play up the international flavor of the Olympic Games by offering a variety of international foods such as

⚽ **Pizza** Order in from a local pizzeria or heat frozen pizzas from the grocery store.

⚽ **Egg Rolls** Heat and serve mini-eggrolls available in the freezer section of most grocery or warehouse stores.

⚽ **Nachos** Fill a paper bowl with tortilla chips. Top with cheese sauce and mild salsa.

⚽ **Pastries** French, Danish, German—There's an international variety of pastries available at bakeries or your neighborhood grocery store.

SonGames 2004 Preview Event Pass: Winners Photo Booth, Decorative Water Bottle, Table Tennis Tournament, Frisbee Discus, Have a Ball, Ball Art, Clothespin Wrestlers, Sporting Dress-Up

Activities

- **Winners Photo Booth** Provide warm-up jackets, various medals and a variety of sports equipment for children and/or their parents to wear. Have them stand on the Medalists' Podium in front of the Stadium backdrop (see "Decorating Ideas" in *Elementary Teaching and Decorating Resources*) and pose with their hands raised in victory to have their pictures taken.

- **Have a Ball** Provide cookies, cupcakes or other round snacks and several colors of frosting: white, orange, yellow, etc. Kids use frosting, licorice strings and decorating icing to make snacks that look like sports balls (baseball, tennis, basketball, soccer, etc.). For a less sweet option, provide rice cakes and a variety of cheese spreads.

- **Table Tennis Tournament** Kids and adults compete in a table tennis tournament. Families and other teams can play in round-robin fashion.

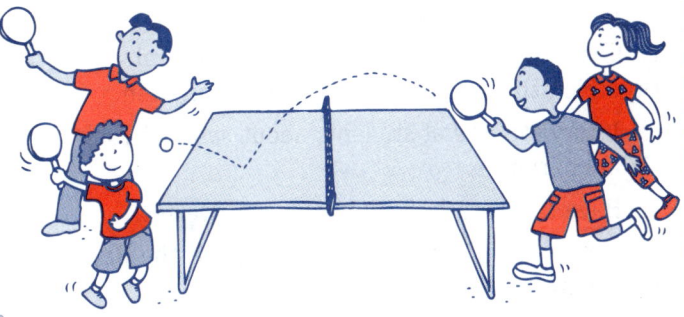

- **Race the Pastor** Enlist the church staff to participate in races. Set up the race course in your parking lot or a playing field at your church. Kids and other family members race against the pastor and/or other staff. Make the race silly by having everyone wear swim flippers, ride tricycles, paddle a wagon with a broom, etc.

- **Decorative Water Bottle** Provide each child with a water bottle and a variety of decorative materials (gel pens, glitter pens, stickers, etc.). Children decorate bottles, printing their names, drawing pictures and other decorations and/or placing stickers.

- **Frisbee Discus** On the ground, spread out a large colorful towel for a target and use masking tape to make a starting line approximately 10 feet (3 m) away. Ask someone to demonstrate the proper way to throw a discus (this could be a current or former high school athlete). Contestants imitate the action using a Frisbee. (Optional: Spray-paint Frisbee with metallic paint.) Prizes can be awarded to anyone who lands the Frisbee in the target. (Note: Play in an open area. Frisbees might get thrown in any direction!)

- **Soccer Dribble** Set up several sports cones in a line, each cone approximately 5 feet (1.5 m) apart. Players dribble a soccer ball between their feet as they weave back and forth between the cones. Players receive a prize after successfully navigating the course.

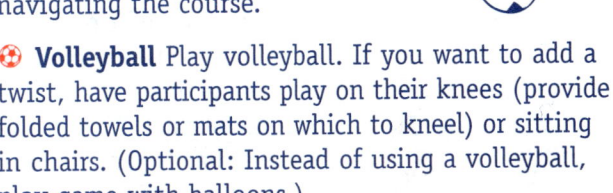

- **Volleyball** Play volleyball. If you want to add a twist, have participants play on their knees (provide folded towels or mats on which to kneel) or sitting in chairs. (Optional: Instead of using a volleyball, play game with balloons.)

- **Ball Art** Pour various colors of tempera paint into separate bowls. In each bowl, place a tennis ball. Participants place a sheet of paper in the bottom of a box and then place a tennis ball covered with paint in the box. Rolling the ball in the box, the participant creates the design of his or her choice. (Optional: Provide a large sheet of butcher paper so that several participants may bounce and roll balls across the paper to each other.)

⚽ **Sporting Dress-Up** Provide a variety of sports clothing and equipment. Participants try on sports clothing over their own clothes and practice using sports equipment.

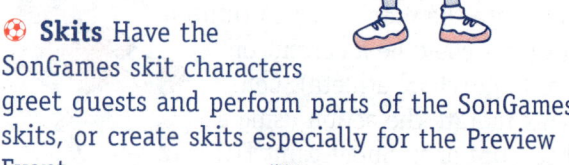

⚽ **Skits** Have the SonGames skit characters greet guests and perform parts of the SonGames skits, or create skits especially for the Preview Event.

⚽ **Clothespin Wrestlers** Give each child two non-spring wooden clothespins and a rubber band. Using markers, children decorate each clothespin to look like a wrestler, drawing on faces, hair and clothing. Next, children wrap a rubber band several times around the two clothespins. Though the rubber bands should hold the clothespin wrestlers together, there should still be a bit of slack. Wind the clothespin wrestlers in different directions, twisting the rubber band between them. Drop them on the floor and watch them wrestle! See which clothespin wrestler pins the other or whether the match is a draw.

⚽ **High Jump** Give each child a piece of chalk—the more colors you use the better! Standing next to an outside wall, each child jumps as high as possible, using the chalk to mark the wall at the highest point he or she can reach.

Closing Ceremony Closing Program

The Closing Ceremony closing program is the culmination of your entire VBS program. It will also be your best opportunity for forming relationships with parents of unchurched children.

The key element of the Closing Ceremony is the skit (see script on pp. 37-40 of the *Assemblies and Skits Guide*). The characters and songs children perform effectively reinforce what children have learned throughout the week. In addition, the program is designed to lead to a presentation of the plan of salvation, giving children and their families the opportunity to hear and respond to the good news of Jesus Christ. This event is one your children, teachers and parents will long remember!

Your Closing Ceremony closing program may also include any of the following ideas:

⚽ Use some of the activity ideas from the "SonGames 2004 Preview Event" article (pp. 24-26) to create an unforgettable event for your church and community.

⚽ Show a "SonGames 2004 Highlights" videocassette or slideshow of everyone participating in the various VBS activities.

⚽ From *Preview Video,* share with parents and children the personal testimonies of several Olympic athletes about becoming a Christian.

⚽ Interview several students about some of their VBS experiences.

⚽ Have students recite Bible memory verses.

⚽ Record a Bible story and pantomime the parts of the story.

⚽ Present the Closing Program Skit (see script in *Assemblies and Skits Production Guide*, pp. 37-40).

⚽ Provide snacks from the Snack Center (pp. 65-70) or other refreshments.

⚽ Guide families on tours of the classrooms. The teachers in their rooms can explain the activities students participated in during the week. Display some of the objects students made or worked with during VBS.

⚽ Ask your senior pastor or other member of the pastoral staff to give a brief welcome and an invitation to attend your church's worship services and Sunday School.

⚽ Set aside a place for kids to get autographs from each other, local athletes and/or skit characters (the *Souvenir Guides* provide space for autographs).

Publicity Guide

Build VBS Interest Within the Church

⚽ **Bulletin Insert** Announce your VBS dates, provide information about preregistration, recruit and promote your VBS by using bulletin inserts.

⚽ *Preview Video* Show the *Preview Video* at children's church or other ministry programs; during a worship service; at Bible studies or prayer meetings; in church lobby, patio or other public area before and/or after church, etc.

⚽ **VBS Video** Show footage filmed at your church during last year's VBS.

⚽ **Posters** Display posters in a variety of locations around your church.

⚽ **Sunday School Visits** Give VBS Coloring Posters to children to color, and display completed posters in church foyer or other high-traffic area. Visit classes to distribute SonGames T-shirts, Plastic Tote Bags or Theme Buttons.

⚽ **Church Website** Add information on SonGames to your church website. Or sign-up for an inexpensive, easy-to-use SonGames website from www.myvbs.com (free with purchase of the Super Starter Kit).

⚽ **Information Booth** Decorate a booth in the church lobby to recruit workers and to preregister children. Display SonGames T-Shirts, Plastic Tote Bags, Theme Buttons, Bookmarks and sample crafts. Make Invitation Postcards and Promotional Flyers available for families to send or take to prospective students and their families. (See the reproducible sample registration card on p. 20.)

⚽ **Theme Buttons and SonGames T-Shirts** Have Sunday School teachers, staff and preregistered students wear VBS items in the weeks leading up to VBS.

⚽ **SonGames Skits** Present one or more of the SonGames skits (see *Assemblies and Skits Production Guide* and the *Teaming Up at SonGames Skit Video*) during a worship service or other congregational event.

⚽ **Music** Play songs from *SonGames* cassette/CD in Sunday School and use as special music in a worship service for several weeks before VBS. Have staff sing a SonGames song during a worship service.

SonGames 2004 Publicity Pieces

√ Bulletin Cover/Insert or Promotional Flyer*
√ Clip Art Sheet*
√ Coloring Poster*
√ Doorknob Hanger*
√ Invitation Postcard*
√ Iron-On T-Shirt Transfer*
√ Large Theme Poster*
√ Outdoor Banner
√ Plastic Tote Bags*
√ *Preview Video*
√ Small Theme Poster*
√ *SonGames* CD
√ SonGames T-Shirts
√ *Student Music Packs* (cassette or CD)
√ Theme Bookmark*
√ Theme Button

*Free in Director's Sample Pack

Reach Out to Children from the Community

⚽ **Outdoor Banner or Sign** Hang the SonGames Outdoor Banner in a visible place outside your church or paint a large sign.

⚽ **Posters** Mount posters (Theme Posters and/or completed Coloring Posters) in businesses frequented by children and their families (grocery stores, laundromats, malls, etc.) and on community bulletin boards.

⚽ **Invitation Postcards** Mail personal Invitation Postcards to last year's VBS students from outside your church. Enclose a cassette or CD of this year's songs. (*Student Music Packs*—cassettes or CDs—are available as an inexpensive alternative to making copies on your own.)

⚽ **Promotional Flyers and/or Doorknob Hangers** Distribute your personalized invitations throughout the neighborhood.

⚽ **SonGames Skits** Present a brief skit and announcement in parks and neighborhoods (see *Assemblies and Skits Production Guide*). A cassette/CD player can be used to play songs from *SonGames* cassette/CD to help attract a crowd.

⚽ **Radio** Use one or both promotional radio spots on the *SonGames* CD to publicize your VBS over local radio stations. After a SonGames introduction, there is background music over which you can announce details about your church's VBS.

⚽ **Newspaper, Television and Other Media** Purchase ad space or use community news space. Use the sample News Release on this page as the basis for a newspaper article about your VBS. Include names of leaders and a photo of some of your staff or the skit characters (Joe Gabbyola, Stella Swift, Brutus Liftsalot and Tumbelina Turnover) for an interesting photo!

⚽ **SonGames 2004 Preview Event** Stimulate VBS interest by holding a Preview Event a week or two before VBS begins. Invite 4- through 12-year-olds and their parents for an afternoon of games, refreshments, crafts, skits and other fun activities (see "SonGames 2004 Preview Event" on pp. 24-26).

⚽ **Preregistration Bonuses** Give a VBS Theme Button or Bookmark to each student who preregisters. Give other VBS goodies to the first 10 (or 20, or . . .) students who preregister.

⚽ **Direct Mail** Send the flyer and/or letter on this page to every family in your community.

⚽ **Prizes** During VBS, give T-shirts to students who bring five or more friends.

⚽ **Parents' Class** Invite parents of VBS students to one or more adult classes held during VBS. Include a get-acquainted coffee time with a variety of special-interest presentations (child development, managing stress, discipline, etc.). Or offer an informal Bible study time. Our recommended adult Bible study for this adult class is *Pressing On to the Prize* (see VBS order blank).

News Release

Send this news release to the city desk of your local newspaper, or use it as a script for radio or television interviews. Adapt the information to fit your church's situation. Send an abbreviated version to your local television station, weekly shopper and appropriate radio stations.

> (Church's name) invites all the children in (name of your community) to join us at SonGames!
>
> "We're ready for a Vacation Bible School your children will never forget," said (minister's name) of (church name). "SonGames creates an atmosphere of fun and excitement where children will have a great time singing, watching skits, creating crafts and playing games. But most important, they'll discover God's love and care for them.
>
> "We're looking forward to sharing this exciting event with the children and parents in our neighborhood. We hope they all will join us at SonGames."
>
> SonGames 2004 begins (date) and continues through (closing date) at (church address) from (opening time) to (closing time). For information, call (church phone number).

Direct Mail Flyer

Use the flyer below to inform families in your church about VBS as well as for outreach to families in the community. As needed, adapt the following to your church's VBS format (Intergenerational VBS, day camp, Backyard Bible School, etc.). Then photocopy the flyer on paper with fun SonGames art (clip art available in Director's Sample Pack, *Teaching and Decorating Resources* or on *Clip Art & Publicity CD*, www.myvbs.com and www.gospellight.com).

> **Be a Good Sport. Join the Team at SonGames 2004!**
>
> We're excited about (name of church)'s Vacation Bible School to be held (dates). This year's program is SonGames 2004, a week of sporting good fun!
>
> At SonGames, children will discover how to live as members of God's team as they Join In! Team Up! Get Strong! Keep On! and Celebrate! We will have a great time with lively songs, skits, crafts, games, Bible stories and snacks—all of the things that make Vacation Bible School so much fun for children.
>
> SonGames can be an inspirational and educational experience for your entire family. Classes for children begin (days and times), and parents are invited to join in (dates and times of family activities). Call us today at (phone number) for registration information, and plan to join us for a great time at SonGames!

Publicity Countdown Calendar

Personalize and adapt this calendar according to your own church's needs, using the items listed on this page as suggestions. The items below set in bold type can be found in the list of publicity ideas.

16 Weeks Before:
- Plan publicity with Director and order publicity materials.
- Put VBS date announcements in a **Bulletin Insert**.

12 Weeks Before:
- Show *Preview Video* in church services and Sunday School classes to develop enthusiasm and to recruit leaders.

8 Weeks Before:
- Hang **Outdoor Banner**.
- Begin placing **Posters** in church building and community.
- Photocopy and distribute **Coloring Posters**.

4 Weeks Before:
- Distribute **Theme Buttons and/or SonGames T-Shirts** to all Sunday School teachers and VBS staff members to wear to church from now through the end of VBS.
- Mail **Invitation Postcards** to prospective students and last year's attendees from outside your church.
- Deliver **Promotional Flyers and/or Doorknob Hangers** throughout neighborhood. Instant e-postcards are available through www.myvbs.com.
- Provide final details regarding preregistration in a **Bulletin Insert**.
- Display completed **Coloring Posters**.
- Arrange to air VBS Promotional Spot on local **Radio** station.
- Use sample News Release and ad on Clip Art Sheet to make contact with local **Newspaper, Television and Other Media**.
- Contact each family in the community using **Direct Mail**.

Publicity Materials

Customize these publicity materials to promote your VBS program. **Tip:** When you send the Follow-Up Postcard, consider enclosing a brochure describing church programs for all ages.

Preview Event Invitation

GET IN THE GAME!
Be a good sport and join the fun at the

Preview the fun of the **SonGames 2004** Vacation Bible School.

PREVIEW EVENT!

THIS EVENT WILL FEATURE MUSIC, GAMES, SNACKS AND ACTIVITIES—ALL WITH A SPORTING THEME.

Come to _____ (place)

_____ (date/time)

DON'T MISS YOUR CHANCE TO BE A PART OF SonGames!

Closing Ceremony Invitation

COME CELEBRATE!

COME CELEBRATE!

CLOSING CEREMONY!

You're invited to the SonGames 2004

Featuring all the teams from SonGames 2004

_____ (place)

_____ (date/time)

Invitation Postcard

JOIN A WINNING TEAM!

You are being recruited to play at !

Please join all your teammates for sporty good fun!

SonGames 2004

_____ (place)

_____ (date/time)

DON'T SIT ON THE SIDELINES—JOIN IN AT SonGames 2004!

Follow-Up Postcard

YOU SCORED BIG WITH US!
Thanks for joining us at

SonGames 2004

WE HOPE YOU AND ALL YOUR FAMILY WILL JOIN US AGAIN AT

_____ (your church name).

Your parents may wish to contact

_____ (contact name)

at _____ (phone)

for more information about our programs for children and families. See ya soon!

Activity Center Guide

The Activity Center Plan is an exciting learning format for your VBS program. Each leader or teacher specializes in only one part of the lesson. Small groups of students led by guides rotate between the various activity centers. One room or outside area is designated for each of the activities your program provides.

The Bible Story/Life Application Center is the core of VBS. Choose from these other centers based on your staff, your facility and the total time available: Opening and Closing Assembly, Crafts, Snacks, Music and Recreation Games, for example. Other centers may include SonGames Training Center, Bible Memory Verse, Bible Story Review or Missions and Service.

Note: Centers are designed to operate best with groups of no more than 16 students. If you have a very large VBS, you may wish to offer more than one of each type of center.

Small Groups and Guides

Students are assigned to small, permanent groups (12 to 16 is the best size). Each group of students visits each center each day (or evening) of the program. Many churches use one adult guide and one youth helper to lead each group and travel with the group to each center.

Leaders or Teachers

Each leader or teacher takes responsibility for one center. The leader remains at the center and instructs each small group as it visits the center. Leaders make adjustments in method and content according to the age level of the students visiting the center.

Note: The Activity Center Plan is recommended for students in grades 1-6. Preschool and Kindergarten Departments remain in a separate area and do not rotate through elementary activity centers. Preschoolers learn best in the security of a familiar classroom (see "Planning Your Early Childhood VBS" on p. 11).

Helpful Hints!

⚽ Predetermine the route each group will travel, including entrances and exits. Have guides walk their routes in advance to become familiar with all locations.

⚽ Establish a signal for letting groups know when it's time to move to the next center.

⚽ Provide labeled tables or other areas where students may leave their belongings throughout the day.

⚽ Set up your centers in classrooms or under tents, awnings or shade trees. Students sit on towels, mats, blankets or picnic benches.

⚽ Provide color-coded name tags or wristbands (available through Gospel Light—see order blank) to identify groups.

⚽ Post a large sign to identify each center.

⚽ Give your centers SonGames names: The Stadium (Assembly Hall) for Opening and Closing Assemblies and Skits, Heroes Hall for Bible Story/Life Application Center, SonGames Training Center for Theme Center. Other centers could be called Swimming Arena, Gymnastics Arena, "Nations of the World" Houses, Playing Field, Locker Room, Sports Center, etc.

The Activity Center Plan—How It Works

The diagram and sample schedules found on the following pages show how the Activity Center Plan can work in your church. Adjust the schedule according to the number of staff and students in your program.

Opening Assembly

The session begins as all students, leaders, guides and helpers meet together for the opening assembly, which includes a welcome, songs and a skit. Encourage guides, helpers and students to sit together.

After the Opening Assembly

Guides and helpers escort their small groups from center to center.

Bible Story/Life Application Center

The leader tells the Bible story and leads students in a life application discussion, using the *Souvenir Guides*.

SonGames Training Center

The leader prepares and leads a theme-related activity that reviews the life application of each day's lesson.

Bible Memory Verse Center

The leader prepares and leads a game that reviews the Bible memory verse and its life application.

Bible Story Review Center

The leader prepares and leads a game that reviews the Bible story.

Missions and Service Center

The leader plans and supervises the teaching about missions and the missions project or other service projects. (Note: Instead of having a separate center, missions could be a part of your opening assembly time. See "Missions and Service Center" on pp. 53-60.)

Recreation/Snack Center*

The Recreation Game Leader prepares and leads the group in high-energy theme-related games. The Snack Leader helps the group in preparing and eating fun theme-related snacks.

Music Center

In a large room or outdoor area, the leader instructs each group in a variety of music activities and teaches the SonGames songs. Information for the Music Center Leader is found in the *SonGames Songbook*.

Craft Center

The leader prepares and guides the students in making a craft project. Information for the Craft Center Leader is found in the *Gold-Medal Crafts for Kids* craft book.

Closing

To conclude, all groups meet together for a closing assembly, which includes announcements, songs and Bible verse review. Guides collect name tags. As students leave, they collect take-home materials from designated tables.

* In our examples, the Recreation Game Center and Snack Center have been combined into one center. For more information about combining these centers see information in "Recreation Game Center" on page 61 and "Snack Center" on page 65.

Diagram for Sample Activity Center Schedule

* You may choose to replace Snacks, Recreation Games, Crafts or Music with one of these four centers.

Activity Center Plan for 36-48 First-Sixth Graders

12-16 children per group (Allow five minutes transition time between centers.)

Centers to set up:
- Bible Story/Life Application Center
- Craft Center
- Activity Center*
- Recreation/Snack Center**
- Music Center

* Activity Center can include SonGames Training Center, Bible Memory Verse Center, Bible Story Review Center or Missions and Service Center.

** In our examples, the Recreation Game Center and Snack Center have been combined. For more information about combining these centers see information in "Recreation Game Center" on page 61 and "Snack Center" on page 65.

Sample Three-Hour Schedule

	Primary	Middler	Preteen
9:00-9:15	Opening Assembly	Opening Assembly	Opening Assembly
9:20-9:45	Bible Story/Life Application	Craft Center	Music Center
9:50-10:15	Activity Center	Bible Story/Life Application	Craft Center
10:20-10:45	Recreation/Snack Center	Activity Center	Bible Story/Life Application
10:50-11:15	Music Center	Recreation/Snack Center	Activity Center
11:20-11:45	Craft Center	Music Center	Recreation/Snack Center
11:50-12:00	Closing Assembly	Closing Assembly	Closing Assembly

Activity Center Plan for 72-96 First-Sixth Graders

12-16 children per group (Allow five minutes transition time between centers.)

Centers to set up:
- Two Bible Story/Life Application Centers (A and B; one for first-second graders, one for third-sixth graders)
- Two Craft Centers (A and B; one for first-second graders, one for third-sixth graders)
- Two Activity Centers (A and B; one for first-second graders, one for third-sixth graders)*
- One Recreation/Snack Center (third-fourth graders will be in this center at the same time)**
- One Music Center (both groups of first and second-third graders will be in this center at the same time)

* Activity Center may include one or more of the following: SonGames Training Center, Bible Memory Verse Center, Bible Story Review Center or Missions and Service Center.

** In our examples, the Recreation Game Center and Snack Center have been combined. For more information about combining these centers see information in "Recreation Game Center" on page 61 and "Snack Center" on page 65.

Sample Three-Hour Schedule

	1st Grade (group a)	1st Grade (group b)	2nd Grade	3rd Grade	4th Grade	5th/6th Grade
9:00-9:15	Opening Assembly	Opening Assembly	Opening Assembly	Opening Assembly	Opening Assembly	Opening Assembly
9:20-9:45	Bible Story/Life Application A	Craft Center A	Recreation/Snack Center	Bible Story/Life Application B	Music Center	Craft Center B
9:50-10:15	Activity Center A	Bible Story/Life Application A	Craft Center A	Activity Center B	Bible Story/Life Application B	Recreation/Snack Center
10:20-10:45	Recreation/Snack Center	Activity Center A	Bible Story/Life Application A	Craft Center B	Activity Center B	Music Center
10:50-11:15	Music Center	Music Center	Activity Center A	Recreation/Snack Center	Recreation/Snack Center	Bible Story/Life Application A
11:20-11:45	Craft Center A	Recreation/Snack Center	Music Center	Music Center	Craft Center B	Activity Center B
11:50-12:00	Closing Assembly	Closing Assembly	Closing Assembly	Closing Assembly	Closing Assembly	Closing Assembly

For More than 96 Students: Offer more than one of each type of center; for instance, SonGames Training Center A and SonGames Training Center B. Both centers have the same activities but in different locations. Offer as many as needed so that groups visiting the center have no more than 16 students.

SonGames Training Center

Play and learn!
Often children are not aware of the direct learning value of an activity, but they participate enthusiastically because they enjoy what they are doing. The following activities provide plenty of teamwork and fun, while helping students learn more about being a member of God's team.

Before beginning the activities, briefly discuss their purpose and what attitudes will help all participants to have an enjoyable time. Remember, the goal is for everyone to have fun while learning.

Tips for Leading Activities

⚽ **Use the conversation suggestions provided with each activity.** They are designed to help students apply the session focus to their everyday lives.

⚽ **Use the adaptations appropriate to the skill level of each class.** As described, the activities are appropriate for third- and fourth-grade skill levels. However, adaptations are provided to simplify each activity for use with first and second graders or to make it more of a challenge for fifth and sixth graders.

Enhance the Theme

The SonGames Training Center is your opportunity to really enhance the VBS theme. Some suggestions that may help you:

⚽ On a television, play a sports-related video with the sound off while children complete activities. Suggested videocassettes include competitions from previous Olympic Games, sports-related movies or cartoons (rated G) or live coverage from the 2004 Olympic Games (if your VBS is running at the same time as the Games).

⚽ If you have extra time in your theme center, or for students who finish early, you can play a videotaped interview with a local athlete. Conduct the interview at the gym, field, pool or other location where the athlete trains. Ask the athlete to explain how he or she trains to compete in his or her sport and why training is so important.

Motto Pennants

Session 1 — Team Flag

Materials Checklist
- Join In! Sports Motto Poster and Flag Symbol Patterns from *Elementary Teaching and Decorating Resources*
- masking tape or tacks
- 9x12-inch (23x30.5-cm) sheets of white construction paper
- fine-tip colored permanent markers
- scissors
- 9x12-inch (23x30.5-cm) sheets of craft foam in three different colors
- lightweight cardboard
- ¼-inch (.6-cm) dowels
- handsaw
- ruler
- whistle
- your country's flag (picture, drawing or flag)
- glue
- tape

Preparation
Display Join In! Sports Motto Poster on wall. On one sheet of white construction paper, draw lines to divide paper into thirds to make flag pattern (see sketch a). Cut the rest of construction paper in half so that there is one half for each student. Cut craft foam sheets in half. Then cut each half into equal thirds to match the flag pattern—at least two pieces of each color for each student. Trace flag symbol patterns onto lightweight cardboard to make several patterns of each symbol. Cut out. For each student, cut a 12-inch (30.5-cm) length of dowel. Find out what the colors (and symbols) on your country's flag represent.

a.

How to Use
Blow whistle. **Welcome, (name of team)! I'm your coach. Each day we'll practice a training exercise from one of the countries represented in the Olympics. Today it's the Denmark Duckwalk.** Demonstrate duckwalk. Students waddle around room perimeter for one to two minutes. Blow whistle again. **Good job, Duckwalkers! Now we're all warmed up and ready to go!** Students sit at tables.

Side-Buster Training Exercise: Each session, get kids laughing with a silly athletic training exercise.
Denmark Duckwalk: Crouch with bent knees and walk, waddling like a duck. Hold hands under arms and flap your wings, too!

Today we're learning about joining a team. Indicate Join In! poster. **No matter what their sport, all Olympic athletes are part of a bigger team—their country's team. At the opening of the Games, each team carries its country's flag into the stadium. Each color (and symbol) means something.** Show flag and explain colors (and symbols).

Your team needs a flag, too, and you can design it! Show white sample flag. Students vote on one of three colors for each part of the flag. Write the color in each section. (Blue/white/blue; red/yellow/green; etc.) Show symbol patterns. Students vote for a symbol and the color they want it to be. Draw symbol on center section of sample flag and write the color. Display flag.

Students replicate the team flag by gluing precut foam sections onto construction paper. They trace the symbol pattern onto the chosen color of craft foam, cut out and glue to flag center. Students may write their team name, their own name or "Join In!" on flags. They tape dowels to flag backs to make poles.

How do you think someone gets to be on an Olympic team? (Practice for many years. Try out. Be one of the best at the sport.) **All of us can be on God's team of people who love Jesus and follow Him. To be on God's team, you don't have to try out—God wants you to just "Join In!"**

Flag Fun: Arrange for an adult volunteer to make a large team flag out of cloth or felt. Once students have designed their flag, the volunteer sews, glues or uses fusible webbing to create the flag and attaches it to a sturdy dowel or piece of PVC pipe. Students take turns carrying their flag on subsequent days of VBS and in the Closing Ceremony closing program on the last day of VBS.

Primary Simplification: Students use one color of fun foam for the flag (which is not divided into sections) and a different color of fun foam for the symbol in the flag's center.

Preteen Challenge: Students choose their own pattern for flags.

Session 2 — Trading Pins

Materials Checklist
- Team Up! Sports Motto Poster and Pin Patterns from *Elementary Teaching and Decorating Resources*
- masking tape or tacks
- colored pencils or permanent markers
- ruler
- scissors
- whistle
- several hole punches
- foil
- oven or several toaster ovens
- oven mitt
- small safety pins
- cookie sheets

For every four students—
- 8x10-inch (20.5x25.5-cm) sheet shrinkable plastic (available from www.shrinkydinks.com)
- four plastic sandwich bags
- four fine-tip black permanent markers

Preparation
Display Team Up! Sports Motto Poster on wall. Draw lines on plastic sheets to create 16 2x2½-inch (5x6.5-cm) boxes; then cut one strip of four boxes for each student (sketch a). Photocopy one copy of pin patterns for each student.

How to Use
Blow whistle. **Welcome back, (name of team)! Ready for some more training?** Demonstrate training exercise. Students walk around room perimeter for one to two minutes. Blow whistle again. Students sit at tables.

Side-Buster Training Exercise
Liechtenstein Link-Up: Students pair up, link arms back to back and walk around room. Say, "Ready, reverse!" Students walk in opposite direction.

Today we're learning about cheering on the members of our team. (Indicate Team Up! poster.) **Sometimes people at the Olympics wear pins to support various teams or events, or to remember the things they saw and did. They collect the pins and trade them with people they meet. Today you'll make pins to remember your time at SonGames and trade with friends at VBS!**

Give each student a plastic strip and a black marker. Students draw in each section of plastic strip to make four pins. Or they use marker and Pin Patterns to trace the design. They may write their team name, their own name or "Team Up!" on pins. Students color in designs, and then cut pins apart. Students use hole punch to punch a hole in one corner of each pin (sketch c).

What are some ways people encourage athletes at a sports event? (Shout cheers. Wear team colors. Hold up signs. Wave flags.) **When might people on God's team need encouragement? What can you do to encourage them?** (Listen to them. Pray for them. Offer to help.) **In the Bible God tells us to encourage each other and help each other live as He wants us to live. God wants us to "Team Up!"**

If using toaster ovens, students place pins on a small piece of foil and leaders place in ovens. Remove from oven and cool a few minutes. Students attach safety pins to holes in pins.

If baking later in a large oven, students use markers to write their names on plastic bags and then place the pins inside. After class, place each student's pins on a foil-covered cookie sheet and use marker to write name on foil. Bake pins according to manufacturer's directions. Attach safety pins and place each student's pins back in student's bag. Pass out during the following session of VBS.

Recycling Option: Instead of shrinkable plastic sheets, use clear plastic deli or bakery containers. Bake in oven at 350°F for 5 minutes.

Trading Time: On the following days of VBS, give students time to trade pins! Prompt them to trade with kids they didn't know before, those who have pins different from their own or those who have birthdays closest to theirs.

Primary Simplification: Tracing patterns can be difficult for first and second graders. Encourage them to draw freely if that is their preference.

Preteen Challenge: Students brainstorm a motto for their team. Students may incorporate their team motto in the design for their pins.

Session 3 — Exhibition Sport

Materials Checklist
- Get Strong! Sports Motto Poster from *Elementary Teaching and Decorating Resources*
- roll of masking tape
- butcher paper and marker, or dry-erase board and marker
- whistle
- several pieces of sports equipment (ball, glove, racket, helmet, goggles, mat, etc.)
- scissors
- newsprint or butcher paper

Preparation
Display Get Strong! Sports Motto Poster on wall. Clear as much floor space as possible. Tape a large sheet of butcher paper on the wall or use dry-erase board.

How to Use
Blow whistle. **Welcome back, (name of team)! Are you ready to get strong? Today we're doing the Finland Flex!** Demonstrate the training exercise. Students walk around room perimeter for one to two minutes. Blow whistle again. Students gather in middle of room.

Side-Buster Training Exercise
Finland Flex: Hold fists out to sides, elbows near body. Flex arms as if lifting weights. Take a giant step forward with each rep.

Not all sports are represented in the Olympics. What are some sports that you think are probably NOT official Olympic sports? (Skateboarding. Scuba diving. Bowling. Golf. Rock climbing.) **At each Olympics, people test out a few new sports. They are called exhibition sports. If enough people become interested in an exhibition sport, it might become a regular part of the Olympics in years to come. Today you will invent a new sport. And who knows? If it becomes popular, you might see it in the Olympics someday!** Show students sports equipment. Brainstorm ways the equipment could be used in a game. Then choose which items will be used. If there are other items needed that students think of, ask volunteers to use masking tape, scissors and newsprint or butcher paper to form them.

Discuss what the rules of the game should be. Write the rules on displayed sheet of butcher paper or dry-erase board. Think of at least three rules. Then play the game! Depending on the sport created, allow students to take turns in positions or in demonstrating the sport.

Coaching Tip: If you have more than one adult leader in the room, divide class into groups of six or more students. Adult leaders guide their groups to create their own game. Then all groups may demonstrate games for the rest of the class.

You thought of some interesting rules! Why is it important to know the rules for a game? (So everyone knows what to do.) **What happens if someone doesn't follow the rules in a game?** (Other players get mad. A penalty or foul is called. Sometimes the game is stopped. The game stops being fun.) **God gives us rules in the Bible to instruct us and to train us, sort of like a coach trains an athlete. If athletes follow their coaches' training rules and practice them, they will continue to get stronger and better at their sports. If we practice following God's instructions in the Bible, we'll get stronger and better at doing what is right! Today we're learning to "Get Strong!"** Indicate Get Strong! poster. **What are some things that will strengthen us to follow God's rules?** (Being with friends who love and follow Jesus. Reading the Bible. Learning about God at church. Praying and asking God to help us.) **God will help everyone on His team to "Get Strong!"**

Primary Simplification: Children use sports equipment that you provided instead of trying to create new equipment.

Preteen Challenge: Instead of creating a new sport as a class, divide students into groups of three to five. Groups develop a new sport as described and then demonstrate it to the other groups.

Session 4: Decathlon Discovery

Materials Checklist
- Keep On! Sports Motto Poster and Decathlon Cards from *Elementary Teaching and Decorating Resources*
- masking tape
- card stock
- scissors
- measuring tape
- three sheets of paper
- marker
- 15-pound or 8-pound weight
- bamboo gardening stake or pole at least 3 feet (.9 m) long
- shoe box or small packing box
- whistle
- beanbag

Preparation
Display motto poster on wall. Photocopy Decathlon Cards onto card stock and cut out. Stack cards into categories. Insert two "God's Promise" cards into each card stack. Clear as much floor space as possible. Use masking tape to create three lines 2 to 3 feet (.6 to .9 m) apart for the target area on the floor and create a fourth line about 10 feet (3 m) from the first line. Print the following words on separate sheets of paper: "Fastest," "Highest," "Farthest." Tape a paper in each section of the target area. Place stacked cards on floor next to paper for each category. Set out the weight, bamboo stake or pole and measuring tape. Set box in a clear area. (Note: These items will be used by students as they complete actions on Decathlon Cards.)

How to Use
Blow whistle. **Today's training exercise is the African Frog Hop.** Students hop around room perimeter for one to two minutes. Blow whistle again.

Side-Buster Training Exercise
African Frog Hop: Squat on the ground and hop like a frog. Say "Ribbit!"

(Name of team), what is our motto for today? (Keep On!) One Olympic event that requires athletes to keep on going is the decathlon. The decathlon isn't just one sport but 10 different events! To win, an athlete tries to run the FASTEST, jump the HIGHEST and throw objects the FARTHEST. The objects they throw are the shot put (a heavy weight), the discus (like a thick heavy plate) and the javelin (a long pole).

To discover more about the decathlon, we'll play a game in which you'll throw a beanbag the way a decathlon athlete throws the shot put. Demonstrate method of throwing a shot put: Bend one arm, holding elbow at side. Hold beanbag in open, flat palm. Then straighten arm, pushing forward and releasing beanbag into the air (see sketch).

Students stand behind line. First player tosses beanbag toward target area. Read a card from the category in which the beanbag lands. Student follows directions on the card. Cards may have a question to answer or an action to do that relates to a decathlon event. Cards may also contain "God's Promise" questions. Continue as time allows or until all students have had a turn.

When have you kept on, even when you wanted to give up? Volunteers respond. **God's promises help us keep on depending on God! It can always help us to remember that He cares for us, loves us just as we are and forgives us!** Students experiment with objects as time allows.

Primary Simplification: Use only the cards with stars on them.

Preteen Challenge: In addition to beanbag, provide two heavy-duty paper plates and a drinking straw. Staple rims of paper plates together to form a discus. Players choose a shot put (beanbag), discus (paper plates) or javelin (straw) to throw at target.

Session 5 — Celebration Medals

Materials Checklist
- Celebrate! Sports Motto Poster and Medal Pattern from *Elementary Teaching and Decorating Resources*
- masking tape or tacks
- yellow or gold card stock
- scissors
- ribbon
- measuring stick
- whistle
- one or more of the following: bunch of celery, sprig of pine needles, olive leaves
- fine-tip markers
- stapler

Preparation
Display Celebrate! Sports Motto Poster on wall. Photocopy onto card stock one copy of medal pattern for each student. Cut one 30-inch (76-cm) length of ribbon for each student. Before class begins, choose a volunteer to play the Winner.

How to Use
Blow whistle. **Come on in, (name of team)! It's the last day of SonGames, and it's time for our final training exercise. What have you seen athletes do when they win or score?** (High-five, jump up and down, hug team members, do victory dances, etc.) **Winning athletes train hard for their sports, but they also have to practice their celebration technique! Let's get in position to do the High-Five Victory Jive!** Demonstrate training exercise. Students do routine for one to two minutes. Blow whistle again. Students sit at tables.

Side-Buster Training Exercise
High-Five Victory Jive: Say, "High-five. To the side. Down low. Way to go!" For each direction, partners slap right hands as indicated in rhyme. On "way to go," partners slap both hands together above head. Repeat several times with students changing partners each time.

It's exciting to win a game or competition. What are some games or competitions you have won? Volunteers respond. **What kind of award or prize did you get?** Volunteers respond. **I think that (name of volunteer playing Winner) did a great job at doing the High-Five Victory Jive and deserves the winning prize!** Ask student to step up and, with a flourish, present him or her with the celery, pine sprig or olive leaves. (If you have all three items, choose three Winners.) **If you were an athlete in ancient Greece, this is a prize you might get for winning a sport!** Athletes received unusual prizes like wild celery, pine branches or crowns made of olive leaves. **What do athletes win at the Olympics now?** (Gold, silver or bronze medals.)

Today you can make medals to remind you to celebrate God's gifts to His team! Indicate poster. **What are some things that God has done for us that we've talked about this week?** (Loves us. Sent His Son, Jesus, so we could be forgiven and join His team. Gives us people to encourage us. Gives us His Word, the Bible, to help us grow stronger. Helps us when times are hard.)

Give each student a medal pattern. On medals, students draw small pictures or write words to show or tell things God has given them. Students cut out medal. Help each student staple ribbon to back of medal to wear around neck.

What did you draw or write on your medal? Volunteers respond. **God has done many great things for us. The Bible says He'll do even better things in the future. God wants us to enjoy what He's given us—but we should never forget that they come from God! Take time to "Celebrate!" by thanking God for all He does for us!**

More Medal Ideas: Provide gold glitter-glue pens or star stickers to give medals added sparkle. For more ideas on how to make medals, see *Gold-Medal Crafts for Kids* craft book.

Primary Simplification: When you photocopy medal pattern onto card stock, enlarge the image by 50 percent.

Preteen Challenge: Provide decorative materials (metallic chenille wires, glitter-glue pens, star stickers, beads, buttons, sequins, synthetic gemstones, etc.). Students decorate one or both sides of medals with decorative materials.

Bible Memory Verse Center

Play and learn! Often children are not aware of the direct learning value of a game, but they participate enthusiastically because they enjoy the game. The following games provide plenty of teamwork and fun, while helping students memorize or review their daily Bible verse.

Before beginning each game, briefly discuss with your group the purpose of the game and the attitudes that will help all participants to have an enjoyable time. Remember, the goal is for everyone to have fun while learning, not to produce winners and losers.

Tips for Leading Games

⚽ **Use the conversation suggestions provided with each game.** They are designed to help students process the meaning of each verse and how it applies to them.

⚽ **Offer a "practice round."** When playing a game for the first time with your class, play it a few times "just for practice." Children will learn the rules best by actually playing the game.

⚽ **Use the adaptations appropriate to the skill level of each class.** As described, the games are appropriate for third- and fourth-grade skill levels. However, adaptations are provided to simplify each game for use with first and second graders or to make the game more of a challenge for fifth and sixth graders.

⚽ **Vary the process by which teams are formed.** Allow students to group themselves into teams of three or four members each. Play the game once. Then announce that the person on each team who is wearing the most (red) should rotate to the team to his or her right. Then play the game again. As you repeat this rotation process, vary the method of rotation so that students play with several different children each time.

Memory Verse Contests

Rather than individual memorization contests, which often discourage children for whom memorization is difficult, challenge your students to work together! For each session of VBS, create a new point goal with prizes for each team. Members of each team earn points toward their team's point goal through Bible verse memorization, attendance, bringing a Bible or friend, etc. Make each point goal achievable by the next session. For example, if by the second session, 25 points have been earned, a prize will be given to the team members. At each closing assembly, announce which teams achieved— or surpassed—their point goal.

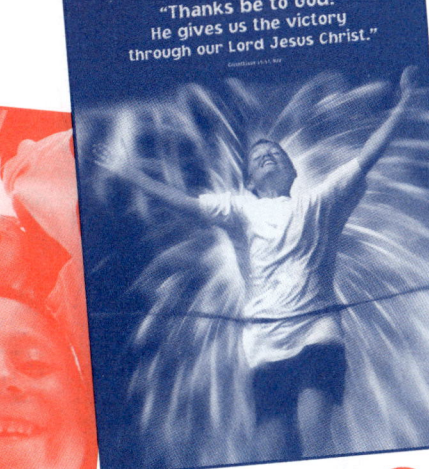

Session 1: Light the Torch

Bible Memory Verse Center

Materials Checklist
- Session 1 Memory Verse Poster from *Elementary Teaching and Decorating Resources*
- masking tape
- marker
- scissors
- five sheets of paper
- five chairs

For each team of four or five students —
- three large sheets of construction paper (one of them red or orange)

Preparation
Display memory verse poster on wall. On each team's sheet of red or orange construction paper, draw a large flame. Write Psalm 100:3 on flame, and then draw lines to separate flame into five puzzle pieces. Cut out flame and cut apart pieces. To make Olympic-like torches, roll sheets of construction paper into two large cones for each team, and tape to secure. Print one of the following names on each sheet of paper: Asia, the Americas, Europe, Africa, Australia. Tape one paper to each of the five chairs. Arrange chairs around perimeter of room.

paper cone torch

How to Use
Before the Olympics begin, runners carry a torch around the world. For our torch relay, each of these chairs represents a continent. **What are the names of some continents in the world?** Volunteers read continents from papers on chairs.

Divide class into teams of four or five players. (If there are fewer than five players on a team, one player runs relay twice.) Each team stands in a separate corner of the room. Give two players on each team a torch and each team member a flame piece to hold. Both Torch Runners put their flame pieces inside the torch. At your signal, Torch Runner 1 on each team runs around room, touches all five "continents," returns to team, pours the flame piece from torch into Runner 2's torch and then hands empty torch to Runner 3, who places his or her flame piece inside. Runner 2 runs the course, returns to team and pours flames into Runner 3's torch. Relay continues with each Runner passing more flame pieces each time around. After the course has been run with all five pieces of the flame in one torch, the team assembles the flame puzzle on the floor. The first team to have all puzzle pieces assembled wins.

Ask winning team to say the verse aloud. **God loves people all around the world and wants them to know that He is God and that Jesus is His Son. He invites us to join His team and accept Jesus' forgiveness.** Have all students say verse aloud together.

Olympic Fact: The five rings on the Olympic flag represent the inhabited continents: Asia, the Americas (North and South), Europe, Africa and Australia.

Primary Simplification: Students suggest names of places to use instead of continents. Instead of passing flames from torch to torch, use only one torch for each team. On his or her turn, each player will place a flame piece in the torch, run around the room, touch each chair with a place name and pass torch to the next player who repeats the actions.

Preteen Challenge: Before cutting flames into puzzle pieces, print one of the following questions or the enrichment verse on the back. After teams assemble flames to say verse, they flip flames over and answer the question or say the enrichment verse.

- **What are some ways that people can know that the Lord is God?** (Go to church or Sunday School. Read the Bible. Pray.)
- **How would we act if we believe God made us and we are His?** (Obey His Word. Talk to Him. Love others. Choose to do what is right.)
- **What are some things that you know about God?** (He made us. He loves us. He is powerful. He sent Jesus so we can be forgiven.)
- "For Christ died for sins once for all . . . to bring you to God" 1 Peter 3:18.

Session 2 — Encouragement House

Bible Memory Verse Center

Materials Checklist
- Session 2 Memory Verse Poster from *Elementary Teaching and Decorating Resources*
- masking tape
- measuring stick
- marker

For each team of six or seven players—
- 16 index cards, all one color

Preparation
Display memory verse poster on wall. On the floor, use masking tape to mark off a 3-foot (.9-m) square for each team (see sketch). On one team's index cards, print Hebrews 10:24, one word or the reference on each card. Use a different color of cards to make an identical set for each team.

How to Use
When you've been away from home, what did you miss the most? Volunteers respond. **At the Olympics, each team has a house that is named for the country they came from, such as U.S.A. House or Canada House. If athletes or other visitors feel homesick, they can gather at their country's house with people from their own country.** Indicate masking-tape squares on the floor. **These squares are your Houses. To play this game, your team needs to collect all its cards and put the verse in order. You can leave your House, but only if you stay connected to someone! Everyone outside of the box has to be connected to someone who is inside the box.**

Divide class into teams. Each team stands inside a House. Assign each team one color of index cards. Scatter index cards on the floor at varying distances from the boxes. At your signal, teams collect their index cards by forming an unbroken chain with at least one team member remaining in the House (see sketch). Students may sit or lie on the floor if necessary to stretch farther, as long as they are connected at all times by hand or foot. As cards are gathered, they are passed back to the House with team members remaining connected. This may require the whole team to move together. When all cards have been gathered, the team places the cards on the floor of the House in correct verse order. They may refer to memory verse poster on the wall. The first team to have their complete verse in order wins. **In this game, could one person have gathered all the cards alone? Why not?** Volunteers respond

Ask winning team to say verse aloud. **"To spur someone on" means to encourage them to do something. This verse is talking about encouraging others to do good things. Sometimes it's hard to do what you know is right. When are times that you know a good thing you can do, but it's hard to really do it?** Volunteers respond. **God gives us other people on His team to encourage us to do good things. What are some things you can do to encourage your friends?** (Pray for them. Offer to help. Help them learn what the Bible says to do.) **This (week) at SonGames, let's remember to encourage each other.** Have students say verse aloud together.

Primary Simplification: For each team, use five to six index cards instead of 16. Print two or three words from the verse on each card. Children take turns leaving their House to retrieve a team card rather than trying to stay connected as described above.

Preteen Challenge: When you repeat game, place a few cards completely outside each team's reach. Once all other cards have been gathered, encourage teams to find a way to retrieve the remaining cards. Help them to discover that it can be done if the two teams work together to form a longer chain.

Session 3 — Strength Training

Bible Memory Verse Center

Materials Checklist
- Session 3 Memory Verse Poster from *Elementary Teaching and Decorating Resources*
- masking tape or tacks
- four sports cones
- bath towel
- nutrition bars
- knife
- large plate
- pitcher of water
- small paper cups
- napkins
- paper
- marker
- two dumbbells

Optional—
- sports drink

Preparation
Display memory verse poster on wall. In each corner of playing area place one sports cone (see sketch). Spread out towel on floor in middle of playing area. Cut nutrition bars into thirds. Place one piece for each student on plate. Place water pitcher, cups, napkins and plate on towel. On one sheet of paper print "Strengthen me" and "5 arm curls." On second sheet of paper print "according to your word" and "Touch toes 5 times." On third sheet of paper print "Run in place and say 'I run in the path' 5 times." On fourth sheet of paper print "of your commands" and "5 jumping jacks." Near each sports cone display one of the four papers. Place two dumbbells next to the first cone.

How to Use
Who has ever practiced or trained to get better at a sport? What are some things you did? Volunteers respond. **Olympic athletes spend years training and practicing. No athlete makes it to the Olympics just by showing up!**

Before training, it's important to stretch out! Lead class in a few simple stretches (reaching toward the ceiling, touching toes, etc.). **Now that you're all warmed up, let's Get Strong!** Divide class into pairs. Pairs line up along one wall of room. Demonstrate how to complete course. Run to one cone, do the exercise printed on the sign while saying verse phrase and then run to next cone. Continue to complete all exercises.

At your signal, first pair begins course. Once they move to next cone the following pair may begin course. After pairs complete course, they stretch to cool down while other pairs complete the course. When all pairs have completed the course, students sit around towel. **After training it's important to eat right and get plenty to drink, so your body will be ready for your next training session.** Pour water into cups and distribute nutrition bar pieces and napkins. Students eat and drink snack. (Optional: Use sports drink instead of water.)

Have a volunteer read verse aloud from poster. **In this verse, "your word" means the Bible. What do you think to be strengthened "according to your word" means?** (To read the Bible, so we can know and REMEMBER what God wants us to do and say in tough situations.) **To "run in the path of your commands" means to practice doing what God tells us in the Bible. When we practice something, we get better at it. What are some of God's commands to practice?** (Obey your parents. Be generous. Tell the truth. Treat others kindly.) **Reading God's Word, the Bible, is one way to get strong so that we can obey God. What are some other ways to get strong?** (Pray for God's help to do what's right. Choose friends who love God and will remind us what is right. Go to church to learn more about God and how He wants us to live.) **Being on God's team doesn't mean everything will be easy. But God promises to help His team to "Get Strong!"**

Primary Simplification: On separate sheets of paper print the sections of the verse but not the actions described above. Walk with students to each cone, repeat the phrase on the cone five times as you lead them in the training activities described in activity.

Preteen Challenge: Instead of assigning pairs, students form pairs on their own.

© 2004 Gospel Light. Permission to photocopy granted. SonGames 2004 Director's Guidebook

44

Session 4 — Turtle Hurdles

Materials Checklist
- Session 4 Memory Verse Poster from *Elementary Teaching and Decorating Resources*
- masking tape
- marker
- measuring stick

For each team of up to ten players—
- ten index cards
- three low hurdles (cardboard boxes, blocks or empty milk cartons)

Preparation
Display memory verse poster on wall. On one set of index cards, print Isaiah 41:10, one or more words or the reference on each card. Repeat with the second set of cards. Use masking tape to mark a starting line on the floor. For each team, starting several feet beyond starting line, place three hurdles in a row, spacing them out across the playing area (see sketch). Divide each team's cards into three random stacks and place one stack on each of their hurdles. Place a length of masking tape on the wall to measure 3½ feet (1 m) above the floor.

How to Use
What do you think would be the hardest event for you if you were in the Olympics? Why? Volunteers respond. **The decathlon is one of the toughest competitions, because you have to finish 10 different track and field events. One event is the hurdles. The athletes run around the track and jump over 10 hurdles, one after the other. The hurdles are 3½ feet (1 m) high.** Indicate masking-tape height marker.

Today you can try a race with hurdles. But these aren't high hurdles—they're more like turtle hurdles! Divide class into two teams. Teams line up behind starting line. At your signal, first player on each team runs to first hurdle, picks up index card and jumps over hurdle and remaining hurdles. Then player turns around and runs back to the team, jumping over hurdles again. Then next player on each team completes the course. Game continues in relay fashion until all cards have been retrieved. Then teams place index cards on the floor in correct verse order. They may refer to memory verse poster on the wall. The first team to have their complete verse in order wins.

Ask winning team to say verse aloud. **What does "be dismayed" mean?** (Be sad or discouraged.) **This verse tells God's promise to us when we might be afraid, sad or discouraged. What is the promise?** (He will be with us. He will strengthen us. He will help us.) **When something goes wrong or we have troubles, the members of God's team shouldn't give up! What can we do instead?** (Trust God's promises. Remember that God is with us and He loves us. Pray, asking for God's strength and help.) **This (week) at SonGames, if you scrape your knee or your team loses a race or someone is unkind to you, remember God's promises and keep on trusting Him!**

Bible Memory Verse Center

Primary Simplification: Divide class into teams of up to eight. Prepare eight verse cards for each team, printing two or more words or the reference on each card. Number the cards in order on the back. Students refer to numbers to help them place cards in order.

Preteen Challenge: Students hold bowls of water on their heads and move slowly and carefully to complete the race, spilling as little water as possible. Be sure to mop up spills with a towel and top off bowls with more water as needed.

Session 5 — Victory Balloons

Bible Memory Verse Center

Materials Checklist
- Session 5 Memory Verse Poster from *Elementary Teaching and Decorating Resources*
- masking tape or tacks
- five large sheets of paper
- markers

For each team of up to ten players—
- balloons in one color, one balloon for each player

Preparation
Display memory verse poster on wall. On each large sheet of paper, print one of the memory verses (Psalm 100:3; Hebrews 10:24; Psalm 119:28,32; Isaiah 41:10; 1 Corinthians 15:57), drawing blanks for three or four of the words in each verse. Spread the papers out on the floor at one side of the room.

Training Tip: Remember to take down memory verse posters from previous sessions before students play this memory verse review game!

How to Use
At the Olympics, there is always a great celebration with music and fireworks to celebrate the winners' victories! What does "have victory" mean? (Win or succeed.) **Today's verse tells us a victory we can celebrate.** Ask a volunteer to read aloud 1 Corinthians 15:57 from memory verse poster. **We can be happy and celebrate because God sent Jesus. Jesus gives us His strength and help to succeed at showing our love for God every day. So let's celebrate our victory and what we've learned this (week) with some balloons!**

Divide class into two teams. Give each team a different color of balloons. Teams line up at least 5 feet (1.5 m) away from the sheets of paper. The first student in each team inflates his or her balloon and pinches the opening closed so that air does not escape. At your signal, players release balloons toward the large sheets of paper.

Players retrieve their balloons. They fill in a blank on the memory verse sheet it landed on or nearest to. Teams help players figure out missing words. Continue game with next players in line. If a player's balloon lands on or near a verse sheet that has already been completed, his or her team says that verse aloud. Continue game until each player has had a turn or until all blanks are filled in.

As members of God's team, we have many reasons to celebrate. What are some of the good things that God does for us as members of His team? (Loves us. Sent His Son, Jesus, so we could be forgiven and join His team. Gives us people to encourage us. Gives us His Word, the Bible, to help us grow stronger. Helps us when times are hard.) **What are ways we can celebrate these good things?** (Sing songs to God. Pray to God and tell Him that we love Him. Give thanks to God. Tell others about God's love.)

Primary Simplification: Instead of inserting blank lines in verses, print complete verse, sizing and spacing words so that they can be covered with one or more Post-it Notes. Provide two different colors of balloons. Inflate one balloon of each color, inserting marble or coin before tying off. Players on each team take turns to bat a balloon toward papers and use Post-it Notes to cover up one word of the verse on the sheets that their balloons land on or near. Team says entire verse together, recalling the covered word(s).

Preteen Challenge: When you prepare memory verse papers, draw blank lines for five or six of the words in each verse.

Missions and Service Center

Doing a missions project during VBS is an excellent way to communicate what it means to live for Christ. At VBS, students learn about God's love for them. By helping others, students have an opportunity to share that love with the world around them.

Fitting a Missions Project into Your VBS

Your missions project can fit into your VBS program in any one of several ways:

⚽ have a five-minute "Moment for Missions" during your opening assembly;

⚽ teach a longer session in individual classrooms; or

⚽ set up a Missions Activity Center, visited by individual classes each day.

Choosing a Missions Project

Consider these factors:

⚽ Visual information about the missionary or special project (such as photos, posters, artifacts, maps, etc.) is important for increasing students' understanding and maintaining their interest.

⚽ Students respond better to meeting a specific need and tangible goal than to giving to a general fund.

⚽ Families who do not regularly attend your church will often be most responsive to a project that assists people with physical needs such as food, clothing or medical aid.

Missions and Service Ideas

⚽ **Racing Toward the Goal Missions Project** As partners in ministry with WORDIRECT, the children in your VBS will help reach thousands of children in China with the Word of God (see pp. 54-55 for project details).

⚽ **Kindness Hoop** Set up a cardboard box with a basketball hoop a few inches above it in your missions center or assembly room. Explain that one way we can show compassion and kindness to our less-fortunate neighbors is by gathering items they need to live. Have students bring in nonperishable food, clothing or other items for a local shelter or food bank your church supports. Each day kids drop items through the hoop and into the box. Students can also help sort the donations into additional boxes or bags and go with you to deliver them when appropriate.

⚽ **Back-to-School Gifts** Contact a local school, community center or family shelter to make arrangements to deliver school and athletic items to children who may not be able to afford them for the coming year. Students may donate school items (sports bags, pencils, notebooks, paper, sports balls, baseball mitts, lunch boxes, erasers, sports socks, crayons, rulers, etc.) or money with which items can be purchased.

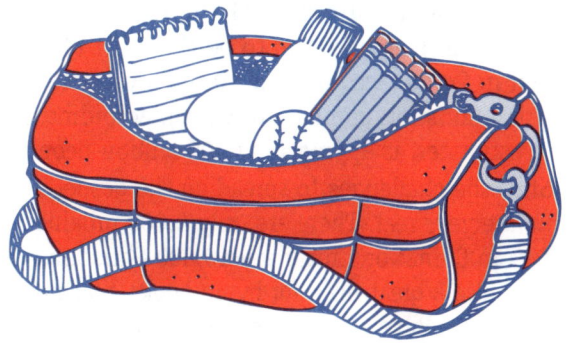

⚽ **Take the Show on the Road** Arrange to perform the Closing Ceremony closing program (pp. 36-40 in *Assemblies and Skits Production Guide*) at a local hospital, retirement home or homeless shelter.

⚽ **Fund-Raising-a-Thon** Hold a jog-a-thon or bike-a-thon to raise money for WORDIRECT, missionaries or another charitable ministry supported by your church.

⚽ **Bag Lunches** Make arrangements ahead of time to deliver bag lunches to a mission, soup kitchen or homeless shelter. Students form an assembly line to prepare sandwiches and place them in resealable plastic bags. Then students place sandwiches, fruit, bags of chips, juice boxes, etc., in brown bags. (Optional: Before placing food items in bags, students decorate bags with markers and/or stickers.)

⚽ Fill a standing locker or a footlocker with offerings of canned food brought in by children. At the end of VBS, donate the food to needy families or a local homeless shelter.

Racing Toward the Goal Missions Project: Team Up with WORDIRECT to Help China's Children

Give your students the opportunity to help children thousands of miles away. As WORDIRECT's ministry partner, you will help reach thousands of children in China—most for the very first time—with the Word of God.

The people of China have experienced great persecution throughout history and there are great limitations to personal and religious freedom still today. Christian materials cannot be openly distributed in public. The importation of Bibles, while not illegal, is prevented. The Chinese government does not want children under the age of 18 taught the Bible. Christians practice religion freely only within church and temple buildings, yet atheists broadcast their beliefs publicly. With all of these restrictions and with limited resources, many Chinese find it difficult to evangelize within their own country.

Despite these adverse conditions, the Christian Church in China is growing. The unregistered or house church network, said to be the heart of the Church in China, accounts for 50 to 80 percent of the total Christian population, which, according to some estimates, is approaching 100 million people.

Still, the challenges to spreading the gospel in China are very real. There are only 3,000 ordained pastors in China: one for every 10,000 Christians. There is also a great need for hymn books, teaching materials and Bible curricula, especially for children.

WORDIRECT's Racing Toward the Goal project responds to these needs in two ways:

⚽ It creates children's Bible teaching materials in Chinese. Based on Gospel Light's curricula, these age-appropriate materials will be carefully adapted to fit the Chinese culture.

⚽ It provides systematic and comprehensive training for Chinese Sunday School teachers in the effective use of these new materials.

Generations of Chinese citizens have lived and died without ever hearing the good news of Jesus Christ. That can change as we teach the children about God's love for them. Together we can give the enduring message of hope to China's children, their families and the generations to come!

After SonGames, send the money raised to WORDIRECT, P.O. Box 3875, Ventura, CA 93006.

WORDIRECT will send your church/VBS a special thank-you to remind the children of the important role they played in world missions.

For more information, contact WORDIRECT at 1-800-737-6071 or www.wordirect.com.

The Great Race

Your VBS children will watch excitedly as each day the runners in The Great Race move closer to the goal!

To create a visual aid, make a poster-board replica of a track stadium (see sketch). Include a finish line on the far right and several hurdles leading up to the goal. Cut out runner figures from different colors of construction paper (pattern available in *Elementary Teaching and Decorating Resources*), one for each session of your VBS.

Choose a reasonable financial goal based on the size of your VBS and write it next to the finish line on your poster. On each hurdle, write dollar amounts to show incremental progress toward your goal, from left to right.

Each day attach a new runner to the poster at a spot along the wall showing the amount of money that has been collected. Encourage your kids to race to the finish—or beyond!

Optional Ideas

⚽ Collect the offering in gold-painted athletic shoes (see p. 7) or in cup-shaped trophies.

⚽ Divide your group into two teams (such as the boys versus the girls) to generate enthusiasm! Assign a goal to each team. The team reaching their goal first wins the competition and members receive a small prize (Peel 'n Press Stickers and other SonGames prizes are available from Gospel Light).

Getting Kids and Parents Involved

⚽ Display a poster with visual aids of the project. A map of China and Chinese translations of the Sports Mottoes are available at www.wordirect.com.

⚽ On the first day of your VBS, explain how The Great Race will be used to show your progress throughout your VBS. Give an update every session.

⚽ Explain what the students' donations will accomplish in terms they can understand. ("The money we raise will help make a book about Jesus. Teachers can use these books to teach children in China.")

⚽ Write a letter to parents about the Racing Toward the Goal Missions Project, or use the sample below. Send the letter home with students after the first session of VBS. Inviting the whole family to participate helps keep students excited.

⚽ Suggest that students earn money by doing jobs for their parents. Some suggestions are included in the sample parent letter. Or encourage students to collect aluminum cans or other recyclable materials to raise money.

Parent Letter

Date
Dear _____,

We are excited to have your child participate in our VBS program. At SonGames they will learn what it means to be members of God's team.

A missions emphasis is included in our VBS program. Our goal is to help children discover the importance of missions and to understand that we can all be involved by praying and supporting special projects.

This year we have selected a project that will reach the children of China with the good news of Jesus Christ. Your child's offering, combined with gifts from children across the country, will be used to produce much-needed Bible curricula in Chinese for the children of China.

The people of China have experienced great persecution throughout history and there are great limitations to personal and religious freedom still today. Christian materials cannot be openly sold in public. The importation of Bibles, while not illegal, is prevented. The Chinese government does not want children under the age of 18 taught the Bible. Yet the Christian Church in China is growing. There is a great need for hymn books, teaching materials and Bible curricula, most especially for children.

We invite your family to help with this important project by praying for China and, if possible, by sharing your offerings, which will be collected at each session of VBS.

The contributions will be more meaningful to your child if your child earns the money him- or herself. Your child might collect and recycle cans, work in the yard, help with household chores or wash the car.

Let's work together to bring the message of God's love!

Thank you,
VBS Director

Getting to Know China

Use these facts about China in your assembly times, during class times or in your Missions and Service Center.

⚽ *Ni Hao* (NEE how) means "Hello" in Chinese. *Zia jian* (ZI jihn) is how you say "Good bye."

⚽ China is on the continent of Asia and is bordered by the Pacific Ocean.

⚽ People in China invented many useful things: the clock, paper, the compass and the wheelbarrow.

⚽ Bike riding is the most common form of transportation in China. Imagine what it would be like to ride a bike wherever you wanted to go. How might that change the things you do each week, alone and with your family?

⚽ China grows more food than any other country. Some of China's biggest crops are rice, tea, potatoes, sugar plants and medicinal herbs.

⚽ The Great Wall of China is a very extraordinary landmark in China. Built over 2,000 years ago as a way to protect the Chinese people from their enemies, the Great Wall is over 4,000 miles long. That's longer than traveling from Los Angeles to New York City! The Great Wall is actually visible to astronauts while orbiting Earth from space.

⚽ Many exotic animals live in China. Some of these animals are the Siberian tiger, the golden monkey and, of course, the panda bear. Giant pandas are black and white bears. Pandas eat up to 12 hours each day and can grow to be 250 pounds. Pandas are tree climbers and can be very shy. Unfortunately, pandas are now on the verge of becoming extinct. The panda is known as a symbol of peace in China.

Chinese Athletes

Visit the WORDIRECT website at www.wordirect.com to download information and pictures of some of China's most recognized athletes (one person for each day), many of whom you might see in the 2004 Olympic Games this summer.

⚽ Wang Zhizhi, men's basketball
⚽ Liu Xuan, women's gymnastics
⚽ Fu Mingxia, women's diving
⚽ Ji Xinpeng, men's badminton
⚽ Sun Wen, women's soccer

Tips for Teachers

⚽ Each missions activity has been carefully designed to incorporate the VBS theme into the missions project. Adapt the ideas as needed so that they are appropriate for your class size, student age, schedule and facilities.

⚽ As you do the activities, share information from the "Getting to Know China" article (see above) and the introductory portion of each activity.

⚽ Remind children that their offerings will help children just like themselves learn about Jesus.

⚽ Pray with your students daily for the needs of China's children. As the children gain knowledge about China, the prayer time will become more meaningful to them!

Missions Activities

Session 1 — Chinese Streamers (20-25 minutes)

Materials Checklist
- map of China (available at www.wordirect.com) and/or world map
- three colors of crepe-paper streamers
- scissors
- measuring stick
- string
- transparent tape
- star stickers

For each student—
- large empty plastic or wooden spool

Preparation
Remove labels from ends of spools. For each student, cut a 1-yard (.9-m) length of crepe paper in each color. Cut string into 18-inch (45.5-cm) lengths—one for each student.

How to Use
Show map of China. **China is the third largest country in the world, with more than 1.3 billion people. China has more people than any other country in the world—one-fifth of the world's population!**

China will have many athletes in the Olympic Games this year. At the Opening Ceremony, the Olympic athletes from China will march in a parade with athletes from countries all over the world! In China, children often wave streamers during parades. Today we're going to make our own Chinese streamers.

Each child folds one end of each streamer into a point (sketch a). Student tapes streamer onto spool and decorates with star stickers. Assist students to thread strings through center of spools and tie knots to secure (sketch b). Students hold spool by the string and wave in the air (sketch c).

This year our VBS missions offerings will help make Sunday School books that are written in Chinese. The books will be given to children in China. We can all Join In! to help the children of China learn about God's love and how to become members of God's team!

a.

b. spool / tape

c.

Enrichment Idea

d. dowel

Enrichment Idea: Instead of holding spool by string, make a long handle by threading spool onto a dowel. Wrap rubber bands around dowel above and below spool so that streamer spins freely (sketch d).

Session 2: Lame Chicken (20-30 minutes)

Materials Checklist
- 20 sticks about 2 feet (.6 m) long
- chalk or masking tape

Preparation
Place 10 sticks on the ground, parallel to each other and about 1 foot (.3 m) apart (see sketch). Use chalk or masking tape to make a starting line about 15 feet (4.5 m) from the first stick. Make an identical course with the other 10 sticks.

How to Use
Today we've been talking about what it means to Team Up! Many different athletes from China will participate in the Olympic Games in Athens, Greece, this year. In addition to Olympic team sports like soccer, gymnastics and badminton, the people of China have team sports of their own. Let's play a team game children in China play. The name of this game is Lame Chicken.

Divide group into two even teams. Teams stand in single file lines behind starting lines. At signal, first player on each team hops up to the first stick and hops over each stick to pick up the last one. Player then hops back over each stick, carrying stick that was picked up, and places stick about 1 foot (.3 m) in front of first stick. Player then hops back to tag next player in line. The next player repeats the process. The first team to have all players complete the course wins.

Note: Players may hop on one foot or two, depending on the age and ability of the group.

Why is being on a team fun? Volunteers respond. **It's fun to cheer our teammates on and to have them cheer for us on our turn to play. One reason to cheer is that God sent Jesus so that people all over the world can be members of God's team. What a great team to join!**

Our missions offerings are a way to team up with children in China. The money we give will help them get Sunday School books written in Chinese. When they learn that God sent Jesus to die for the wrong things that we do, they can choose God's love and forgiveness and become members of God's team!

Missions and Service Center

Session 3 — Chinese Chocolate Haystacks

Materials Checklist

Food Items—
- 12-oz. pkg. butterscotch pieces
- 12-oz. pkg. chocolate chips
- 1/2 tsp. vanilla
- 3 cups chow mein noodles

Utensils—
- measuring cups
- large saucepan
- large bowl
- wooden spoon
- spoons
- waxed paper
- cookie sheet
- napkins

Optional—
- 1 cup chopped walnuts or peanuts

How to Use

Today we've been talking about ways to Get Strong! One way athletes get strong is by eating high-energy food, like spaghetti. Raise your hand if you like spaghetti. *Students respond.* **Most people think that spaghetti noodles come from Italy, but Marco Polo brought noodles to Italy from China. Some Chinese noodles are boiled, but sometimes they are fried to make them crispy. They're called chow mein noodles. Today we'll make a sweet snack using chow mein noodles.** Children place butterscotch pieces, chocolate chips and vanilla in saucepan. Cook on low heat until melted. Remove from heat. (Optional: Place butterscotch pieces and chocolate chips in a microwave-safe bowl and microwave to melt.)

Children place chow mein noodles in large bowl. (Optional: Mix nuts in bowl with chow mein noodles.) Pour melted candy over chow mein noodles; stirring to coat well. Drop heaping spoonfuls of mixture onto waxed-paper-lined cookie sheet. Let stand until firm. (Note: To speed up firming process, refrigerate snacks.)

God gives us food to help us grow strong physically. What does God give us to help us grow strong as members of His team? (Other teammates to help us. The Bible, His instructions.) **By helping children in China have Sunday School books in their own language, we're helping them grow as members of God's team. We're helping our Chinese teammates!**

Missions and Service Center

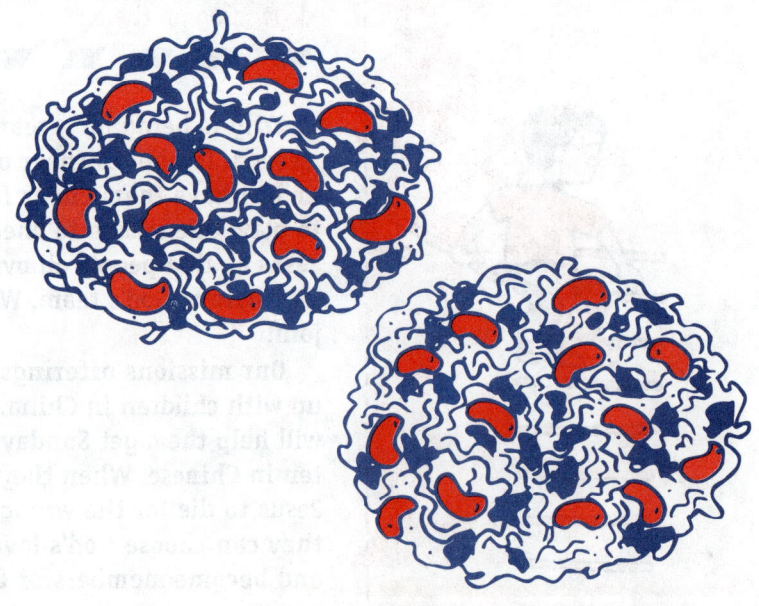

Allergy Alert: Post a note alerting parents that snacks will be served during your VBS and asking for allergy information. Many churches ask that such information be given on their VBS registration forms. This is especially important when serving snacks to younger children who may not be aware of or able to warn teachers about their allergies.

Session 4: Ping-Pong-athlon (15-20 minutes)

Materials Checklist
- six sheets of construction paper
- marker
- three or four Ping-Pong paddles
- masking tape
- measuring tape
- large shallow cardboard box
- beach towel or small blanket

For each student—
- Ping-Pong ball

Optional—
- stickers (Peel 'n Press Stickers available from Gospel Light)

Preparation
Print numbers 1 to 5 on separate sheets of construction paper. Print "Keep On!" on the remaining sheet of construction paper. Place each of the numbered sheets in a different area to make five activity stations. Next to the "1" card, place the Ping-Pong paddles. Next to the "2" card, make a starting line from masking tape. Make another masking-tape line 10 feet (3 m) from the starting line. Place the sheet of construction paper with "Keep On!" printed on it inside the shallow cardboard box. Make a masking-tape line next to the "3" card and place box 10 feet (3 m) away. Place beach towel or small blanket 10 feet (3 m) from the "4" card.

How to Use
Hand each student a Ping-Pong ball. **How many of you have played Ping-Pong?** Students respond. **Ping-Pong is another name for table tennis, and table tennis is an Olympic sport. It is one of the most popular sports in China, and the Chinese people are very proud of their athletes' abilities. During the 2000 Olympic Games in Sydney, Australia, the Chinese team won four gold medals, three silver medals and a bronze medal!**

Explain and demonstrate to students what to do at each of the five stations.

1. **Use the Ping-Pong paddle to bounce the ball in the air 20 times in a row** (or 10 times or 5 times, depending on the age and ability of your group). **If you drop the ball, start again.** (See sketch a.)
2. **Beginning at the starting line, blow the ball over the opposite line. Don't use your hands!** (See sketch b.)
3. **Standing at the starting line, toss your ball into the box. If you miss, keep on trying!** (See sketch c.)
4. **Standing at the starting line, bounce** (or roll) **your ball onto the (beach towel). If it rolls off, try again!** (See sketch d.)
5. **Balance the ball on two fingers. Hold it there for a count of 20** (or 10 or 5). **If you drop it, start over.** (See sketch e.)

Not all of these tasks were easy to do. When something is hard, we can keep on trying. We can trust God to help us Keep On! when things are hard. This is good news we can share with children in China. Our VBS missions offerings will help to get Sunday School books for children in China. The books will be written in Chinese, so they can understand about God's help and His love for each one of us.

Missions and Service Center

Session 5 — Dancing Lion Toy

Materials Checklist
- Lion Head and Lion Tail patterns
- card stock or poster board
- scissors
- 9x12-inch (23x30.5-cm) colored construction paper
- markers
- glue or tape

For each student—
- 2 wooden bamboo skewers or drinking straws

Optional—
- yarn
- glitter
- wiggle eyes

Preparation
Enlarge Lion Head and Lion Tail patterns at 200 percent onto card stock or poster board and cut out to make patterns. Repeat to make several copies of each pattern. Cut sheets of construction paper into thirds, creating one piece for each student.

How to Use
The Chinese New Year, also known as the Spring Festival, is China's biggest holiday. As part of the Chinese New Year celebration, people buy presents, decorations, special foods and new clothing. The New Year's Eve supper is a feast with all the members of the family getting together. At midnight, the sky is lit up by fireworks. The fireworks remind everyone that the old year is ending and the new year is beginning. Traditionally, on Chinese New Year, two people wear a huge lion or dragon puppet costume. Let's make a paper lion version of this puppet.

Students trace the Lion Head and Lion Tail onto sheets of construction paper and cut out. Then they choose a piece of construction paper you prepared ahead of time. Students accordian-fold the paper and tape a lion piece to each end. Students decorate lions with markers. (Optional: Students cut pieces of yarn for a mane and attach to lion. They use glitter and wiggle eyes to decorate lions.) When decorated, students tape one bamboo skewer or drinking straw to the front piece and the other to the back.

We've been talking today about celebrating. The people in China celebrate the Chinese New Year. What are some important celebrations in our country? Volunteers respond. **At the Olympics, people celebrate winning, but they also celebrate with people all over the world who come together and learn more about each other. Our missions offerings will help the children in China learn more about God. And that's a wonderful reason to celebrate!**

Missions and Service Center

Lion Head

Lion Tail

Appendix A

Intergenerational VBS Guide

Bring Families Together for SonGames 2004!

In today's busy, fragmented world, few families have regular opportunities to work, learn and laugh together. Even less common for most families are special times of exploring solid, practical guidance from God's Word for daily family living. An Intergenerational SonGames VBS offers the families of your church and community an opportunity to grow together in a fun and exciting format. Instead of the traditional VBS, which may or may not involve adults, an Intergenerational VBS keeps family members together for part—or even all—of the activities. There are many ways to adapt your SonGames materials to effectively involve families. For example, you may want to

- plan the Opening Assembly for families and then have family members go to their age-level groups;
- plan one or more family activities in addition to the Opening Assembly, with a shorter time in age-level groups (see Option A, p. 74);
- keep families together for the entire session (see Option B, p. 74).

Whichever approach you prefer, in these pages you'll find the help you need to make your Intergenerational SonGames a success.

Family Groups/Teams

Assign each family to a group of four to six families (12 to 16 people). The number of family groups you form will depend on your total attendance, as well as the space and staff you have available. Let each family group choose their own name (Soccer Superstars, Daring Divers, Rapid Runners, Swell Swimmers, etc.). Choose a distinctive color and symbol for each family group's name tags.

Family Activity Centers

Determine which activities you will offer for family groups (Family Activity Centers) and which will be for age-level groups. We provide adaptations for families for the SonGames Training Center, but you can adapt any of the other centers as well.

Set up activity centers as described in the Activity Center Guide beginning on page 31. Family groups will rotate between family activity centers and age-level activity centers according to a schedule you create.

Guides/Coaches

Each family group should have one or more Guides (see p. 15) who lead the group to the appropriate centers. These Guides help families get to know each other better and assist parents in involving their children in activities.

Family Activity Center Leaders

Enlist at least one person to direct and/or teach each family activity center. These friendly leaders remain at their centers and work with each group as it rotates through.

Note: The intergenerational approach is recommended for children ages four and up and their families. Younger children often find it difficult to participate effectively in a program where they are expected to rotate from center to center.

How It Works

The schedules and ideas on these pages show how an Intergenerational VBS can work in your church. Choose the option that fits your situation best and then adjust as needed.

Registration/Arrival

As families arrive, they are assigned to a permanent group, introduced to their Guide and are given or have the opportunity to make their group name tags.

Opening Assembly

The session begins as everyone meets together for the Opening Assembly, which includes a welcome, songs and a skit.

To get all ages participating right from the start,

1. prepare two or three families (or an entire family group) in advance to help teach a SonGames song (including any motions);
2. assign parts of songs to different family groups or family members (dads, moms, all kids,

dads and daughters, moms and sons, etc.); and/or

3. invite a family from each group to participate in a simple stunt or contest that involves the whole family. Use a different stunt each day. For example:

⚽ line up each family and see how many sports balls they can pass down their line in 30 seconds;

⚽ have a three-legged race;

⚽ race to put words of the session's Bible Memory Verse in the correct order;

⚽ have families race to dress a member of their group as a soccer player (or a player of another sport).

After the Opening Assembly

Guides lead their family groups to the Family Activity Centers and other centers according to your chosen schedule. Use as many centers as your schedule and facilities allow. Have a predetermined signal to indicate when it is time to rotate to the next center (see suggested transition ideas in "Winning Ideas" on p. 6).

SonGames Family Training Center

Lead family groups in doing the activities and crafts described in the SonGames Training Center, pages 35-40. Below are some suggestions to adapt the activities for your family groups.

Side-Buster Training Exercise: Each session, get families laughing with a silly athletic training exercise. Make sure there is room around the perimeter of the room for everyone to participate.

Session 1—Team Flag (p. 36)

Side-Buster Training Exercise Lead family groups to do the Demark Duckwalk. Keep it lively by challenging the adults to keep up with the kids!

Activity Families then work together to make a family flag as described in "Team Flag." Instead of individual flags, encourage families to create a family flag on a large sheet of poster board. Provide a variety of cookie cutters in addition to the Flag Symbol Patterns from *Elementary Teaching and Decorating Resources* for families to use to trace and then cut out designs from construction paper or fun foam. Encourage each family to come up with a family motto ("All for one and one for all;" "The family that prays together stays together;" etc.) to inscribe on their flag.

Session 2—Trading Pins (p. 37)

Side-Buster Training Exercise As families pair up for the Liechtenstein Link-Up, make sure that pairs are made up of people of similar heights. This is more important than having family members stay together. Also it can serve as a way for members of different families to get to know each other.

Activity Challenge families to come up with a family cheer as they make their trading pins. Some sample cheers are "Hey, hey, we're the Haysteads!" "Our name is Fiano. We all play piano."

Session 3—Exhibition Sport (p. 38)

Side-Buster Training Exercise Challenge adults and older children to hold dumbbells, water bottles or books while doing the Finland Flex.

Activity Each family makes up an exhibition sport. Provide large sheets of paper on which each family can list their rules. Set aside at least half of the time you have available so that families can explain and demonstrate their sport.

Session 4—Decathlon Discovery (p. 39)

Side-Buster Training Exercise Instead of simply hopping for the African Frog Hop, families play Leap Frog around the perimeter of the room.

Activity Families decide ahead of time which area they wish to shoot for. Lining up at the starting line, the families throw their beanbags like shot puts at the same time. Read a question from the category in which most of the family members' beanbags land.

Session 5—Celebration Medals (p. 40)

Side-Buster Training Exercise Family groups add their own motions to those given in the High-Five Victory Jive. Allow two or three minutes for families to discuss and agree on the added motion. Then, members from families intermingle to perform the jive several times, changing partners with each repetition.

Activity In addition to the Medal Pattern, for each family member prepare another card stock circle the same size as Medal Pattern. On the second card stock circle, family members write their family motto and/or draw a replica of their family flag. Instead of cutting ribbon ahead of time, provide a variety of ribbons. Families select a color of ribbon, cut a 30-inch (76.5-cm) length for each member, sandwich ribbon ends between card stock circles to make a medal with a front and a back, and staple to secure.

Bonus Idea: In addition to or instead of making the medals described above, families create medals for each member of the family: "Longest Sleeper-In," "Fastest Dishwasher," "Warmest Hugger," etc.

Crafts

The *Gold-Medal Crafts for Kids* craft book has a wide variety of craft ideas, including many that easily lend themselves to being done as a family project rather than an individual one. (You may prefer to have crafts done in age-level groups.)

Recreation/Snacks

"Snack Center" (on pp. 65-70) contains a good selection of snack ideas that allows families to work together in preparing and enjoying some tasty treats. The leader for this center provides the snack supplies and instructions; then families do the rest. If you need additional activities to fill this time, you may lead families in playing one of the recreation games described in "Recreation Game Center" on pages 61-64. (You may prefer to do these activities in age-level groups.)

Bible Story/Life Application

The leader in charge of the Bible Story/Life Application Center presents each day's story from the *Middler Teacher Book* to each family group. To help families talk about ways that the Bible story applies to them today, read the student *Souvenir Guides*. Prepare some questions and/or activities for each family group to work on together and some for each family to work on among themselves. Or reinforce the Bible lesson using the Bible story review game or Bible memory verse game in the *Middler Teacher Book* or the *Director's Guidebook*.

To keep the attention of the various age levels present during the story time, consider these ideas:

⚽ Arrange seating in a wide semicircle to avoid having any of the younger students in the back. Families should sit together so that parents can help their children focus on the story presentation.

⚽ Keep the story time brief. With four- and five-year-olds in the group, a story should not exceed five minutes.

If you choose to do part of the session in age-level groups, students may complete activities in appropriate age-level *Souvenir Guides* to review story and application, while parents may enjoy engaging in the recommended adult Bible study, *Pressing On to the Prize*.

Closing

To conclude, all family groups and activity center leaders meet together to wrap up with singing, Bible memory verse review and an invitation to the next session. Guides collect name tags and help families gather crafts and other items to be taken home.

Intergenerational Teaching Tips

Most of your families and leaders are likely to have only limited experience with participating in family-learning activities along with other family groups. Family groups that have a wide range of age levels pose some unique challenges for those who are less familiar with the dynamics of a mixed-age group. A few helpful guidelines for teaching family groups:

⚽ Use a signal to get everyone's attention before you speak. Blowing a whistle, sounding a musical note, ringing a bell, quickly flashing the lights off and on, and making a large gesture (holding both arms straight overhead) are all effective ways to get attention without shouting. Explain your signal and practice it several times with the group. Ask the students to help their parents learn to respond to your signal.

⚽ Talk to all age groups. If a leader focuses on the four-year-olds, older students and adults will tune out. If a leader focuses on the parents, the students will get restless. Remember, even four-year-olds can understand over 90 percent of normal adult conversation. The following tips can help you talk to all age groups:

1. Be brief, keep sentences short, use ample gestures and facial expressions, and vary the pitch and volume of your voice.

2. Intentionally refer to different age and grade levels, as well as specific families, in your talk. ("I bet the third graders already figured that out." Or "Jesus wasn't born in a nice clean hospital like you may have been, Claire.") When you need to say something specifically to parents, you may ask the students to cover their ears because you want to tell their parents a secret. Of course, the kids will suddenly become highly attentive!

⚽ Enlist parents as partners in "crowd control." Many parents who are perfectly capable of controlling their children in normal situations will abdicate that responsibility when someone else is the leader. And many leaders are reluctant to deal with a behavior problem when the parents are present. Explain to parents that in a group family-learning situation, parents and leaders must take joint responsibility for guiding children. For example say, "Because there are lots of people and lots of activities, it is not always possible for a parent or leader to see everything. We must help each other in giving good directions and enforcing limits so that we can all have a relaxed, enjoyable time together."

⚽ When families are working together, encourage parents to allow their children to do as much of the work as possible. Because of the variance in students' age levels, some parents will need to do more "helping" than others. Remind parents that the goal is not to see which family produces the most attractive project or wins in a game or activity. The goal is for families to enjoy working and learning together.

⚽ When families are given a question to discuss, alert parents to share brief answers and experiences that encourage children to participate. Lengthy explanations or stories tend to stifle children's interest, so parents should keep their comments as concise as possible.

⚽ Provide an opportunity for families to pray together during the Bible Story/Life Application part of the session. Instruct parents to keep the prayers very simple so that even the youngest child can participate fully. You may suggest the following helpful approaches, which can also aid parents who are uncomfortable with praying aloud:

1. Let a family member suggest one thing to pray about; then each family member offers a one-sentence prayer of agreement about that. ("I'm glad Blake is thankful for our family.")

2. Invite each family member to tell God one thing for which he or she is thankful or to ask Him for one thing.

3. Each family member thanks God for the family member to his or her right.

4. One family member volunteers to pray; then they all join in saying "amen" ("so be it" or "let it be done") at the end.

Intergenerational Schedule Options

Option A: Family Opening, Family Activity Plus Separate Age-Level Activities
Sample 90- to 120-Minute Schedule

	Children	**Parents**
15 Minutes	Opening Assembly	Opening Assembly
20-30 Minutes	SonGames Training Center	SonGames Training Center
40-60 Minutes	Age-Level Groups for Snacks, Games, Bible Story/Life Application	Adult Bible Study, *Pressing On to the Prize*
15 Minutes	Closing Assembly	Closing Assembly

Option B: All Family
Sample 90- to 120-Minute Schedule

	Group 1	**Group 2**	**Group 3**
15 Minutes	Opening Assembly	Opening Assembly	Opening Assembly
20-30 Minutes	SonGames Training Center	Recreation/Snack	Bible Story/Life Application
20-30 Minutes	Recreation/Snack	Bible Story/Life Application	SonGames Training Center
20-30 Minutes	Bible Story/Life Application	SonGames Training Center	Recreation/Snack
15 Minutes	Closing Assembly	Closing Assembly	Closing Assembly

Notes
1. Suggested times in each block include five minutes of transition time from the previous activity.

2. Two- and three-year-olds remain in a separate area, following their own program schedule.

3. If you form more family groups than shown on these charts, two or more groups can be doing the same activity at the same time in different areas or rooms. Except for the opening and closing assemblies, avoid grouping too many people together for any of the activities. Participation of each person will be greatest and potential behavior problems minimized when family groups are kept to four to six families (12 to 16 people).

Appendix B

Backyard Bible School

What Is a Backyard Bible School?

Backyard Bible School is similar to traditional Vacation Bible School, but a backyard location affords some unique merits:

⚽ It provides a welcoming place close to home for unchurched children to learn about Jesus.

⚽ It enables Christians to minister within their own neighborhoods.

A Backyard Bible School works because kids love to be invited into a neighbor's home with all their friends. They enjoy the relaxed setting because it's a "come as you are" affair where bare feet and play clothes are the usual attire. The parents are happy because their children will be busy for over two hours. The home offers a special hospitality and proximity that is often not possible in an institutional setting.

What About Facilities?

The home need not be large, but it should have a few basics:

⚽ a place to tell the story, such as a family room, patio or shaded lawn;

⚽ a separate place to do crafts, such as a patio, garage or basement (a table or two in this area is a good idea but not necessary; students can work while standing at the table, or they can work on the floor);

⚽ a place for serving refreshments (this can be the same area as used for crafts);

⚽ a place to play active games such as a front yard, backyard or driveway (if necessary, a nearby park or common area will do).

How Does a Backyard Bible School Work?

It begins with a Christian making his or her home available for a given week(s). Then a teacher and at least two adult or youth helpers join to make up a teaching team. They study and prepare the SonGames learning materials.

Monday comes as usual, but this week will be very special. The members of the teaching team arrive early for prayer. The hostess has prepared snacks and sent out a few kids to "round up the gang." The morning will include a Bible story with life application, Scripture memorization, singing, crafts, refreshments and games. Many students will hear about Jesus for the first time. Many will become Christians.

Who Are the Workers?

⚽ **The Hostess** It can't be done without a hostess. Her home is the focal point of all activity; her church is the resource, and her neighborhood is the mission field.

Her natural hospitality and friendliness established among her neighbors will ensure good attendance. If she is new in the neighborhood, this will be an opportunity to meet neighbors and establish rapport.

The specific responsibilities of a hostess are

1. to invite the other teaching team members to her home a week ahead of time to look over the facilities and make plans;

2. to give out the invitations to neighborhood families;

3. to have her home in order;

4. to plan and serve the refreshments;

⚽ **The Teacher** The teacher's influence is primary in the lives of the students. Therefore his or her spirit, knowledge of the subject matter and knowledge of how to deal with students will either "make or break" the week for everyone else involved. It is the teacher's job to take the reins on Monday morning as the first student arrives. The teacher's smile and friendly, decisive directions will help each student feel wanted, happy and cooperative. The helpers are available to do the jobs that the teacher delegates to them. When the teacher is able to encourage a spirit of love and cooperation among the students, as well as the mutual respect of all involved, this spirit lives on in the minds of the students—even years later.

The teacher's specific responsibilities are

1. to know what is scheduled to happen next;

2. to learn the Bible story and present it to the students;

3. to delegate or lead other activities such as crafts, recreation games and singing;

4. to lead the planning meeting at the home of the hostess.

⚽ **The Helpers** In most cases two helpers are needed. If more than 20 students are expected, enlist at least one more helper. Helpers can be anyone with a love for children and a willing spirit. Teenagers and grandparents alike enjoy helping. Some helpers may have special abilities or interests in songs, crafts or recreation games.

It is important for helpers to show their personal interest by participating with the students. They should talk with students as they arrive and learn their names. Helpers need to guide students in the learning activities, sing with them, play games with them and enjoy the story with them. The helpers may be assigned to participate in the SonGames skits. The general rule for helpers is to follow the lead of the teacher in charge. However, the teacher may ask a helper to lead an activity.

A helper's specific responsibility begins at the meeting in the home of the hostess and then will depend on the specific jobs assigned by the teacher.

Backyard Bible School Countdown Calendar

8 Weeks:
⚽ Educate the congregation with write-ups in bulletin or newsletter.
⚽ Order course supplies.

4 Weeks:
⚽ Enlist a hostess, teacher and two (or more) helpers.
⚽ Set the dates, time and place of the Backyard Bible School.

3 Weeks:
⚽ Make up a kit of materials (give *Teacher Books* and *Helper Handbooks* to teacher and helpers).

2 Weeks:
⚽ Hostess calls the team to schedule the meeting at her home the next week.
⚽ Teacher prepares to delegate responsibilities at the meeting.

1 Week:
⚽ Team meets at the home of the hostess. Teacher delegates responsibilities.
⚽ Team members prepare for their parts.

Sample Schedule

20-30 Minutes	Team Devotions and Preparation
10 Minutes	Opening Assembly
20-30 Minutes	Bible Story and Life Application
20-30 Minutes	Bible Story Review Game, Bible Memory Verse Game or SonGames Training
20-30 Minutes	Recreation/Snack
20-30 Minutes	Crafts
10 Minutes	Closing

© 2004 Gospel Light. Permission to photocopy granted. SonGames 2004 Director's Guidebook

Appendix C

Course Overview—King James Version

Bible Theme: Paul's Adventures
Theme Verse: *But thanks be to God, which giveth us the victory through our Lord Jesus Christ.* 1 Corinthians 15:57

Session	Bible Story	Focus	Bible Memory Verse
1 JOIN IN!	**God Picks Paul** Acts 9:1-22	God wants me to be on His team and, through Jesus, offers me His love and forgiveness.	"Know ye that the Lord he is God; it is he that hath made us, and not we ourselves; we are his people, and the sheep of his pasture." Psalm 100:3
2 TEAM UP!	**God's Team Helps Paul** Acts 9:20-30; 11:19-26; 13:1-3	God gives me a team so that we can cheer each other on.	"And let us consider one another to provoke unto love and to good works." Hebrews 10:24
3 GET STRONG!	**Paul Stays Strong** Acts 16—18:11	God gives me strength to obey His instructions.	"Strengthen thou me according unto thy word. I will run the way of thy commandments." Psalm 119:28,32
4 KEEP ON!	**Paul Weathers the Storm** Acts 27	God promises to help me through tough problems.	"Fear thou not; for I am with thee: be not dismayed; for I am thy God: I will strengthen thee; yea, I will help thee." Isaiah 41:10
5 CELEBRATE!	**Paul Reaches His Goal** Acts 28	I can celebrate the good things God gives me as a member of His team.	"But thanks be to God, which giveth us the victory through our Lord Jesus Christ." 1 Corinthians 15:57

Gospel Light's SonGames 2004 Index

Activity Center Guide	31
Backyard Bible School	75
Bible Memory Verse Center	41
Bible Story Review Center	47
Course Overview	2
Course Overview—KJV	77
Director's Countdown Calendar	22
Director's Planning Guide	10
Intergenerational VBS Guide	71
Materials Preview	8
Missions and Service Center	53
Publicity Guide	27
Recreation Game Center	61
Snack Center	65
Snapshot of SonGames 2004	4
Special Events	23
SonGames Training Center	35
VBS Questionnaire	79

We'd Like to Know What You Think

Gospel Light's SonGames 2004

After VBS is over, would you please take a few moments to complete this questionnaire?
Once you're finished, fold it over so that the address side is on the outside and just drop it in the mail. Thank you!

Your name _____
Your title _____
                                    Staff/Volunteer (circle one)
Church name _____
Pastor's name _____
Church address _____
City, State _____
Zip _____
Denomination _____
Average weekly church attendance _____
Church fax: (_____) _____
E-mail address _____

The optional information below will help us meet your needs.
Education completed _____
How many Christian books do you buy each year? _____

1. How did you first learn about Gospel Light's SonGames 2004 Vacation Bible School?
   ❏ Sunday School convention
   ❏ Friend told me
   ❏ Phone call from Gospel Light
   ❏ Brochure in mail
   ❏ Card-pack card
   ❏ VBS workshop
   ❏ Christian bookstore
   ❏ Magazine advertisement
   ❏ Other (please specify) _____

2. What teaching format did you use for elementary students?
   ❏ Self-contained classroom format
   ❏ Activity Center format
   ❏ Modified Activity Center format
   ❏ Other (please explain) _____

3. Please tell us why you chose Gospel Light's SonGames 2004. On a scale of 1 to 4, rate each of the criteria listed below. (1=least important; 4=most important)

IMPORTANCE	LEAST			MOST
Bible content: Paul's Adventures	1	2	3	4
Provided gospel presentation	1	2	3	4
Creative/captured imagination	1	2	3	4
Different from other courses	1	2	3	4
SonGames 2004 theme	1	2	3	4
Teacher Book content/format	1	2	3	4
Teaching and Decorating Resources	1	2	3	4
Music	1	2	3	4
Student guidebook content/format	1	2	3	4
Director's materials to organize program and recruit teachers	1	2	3	4
Craft book	1	2	3	4
Skits	1	2	3	4
Cost/value	1	2	3	4
Promotional helps	1	2	3	4
Different from regular Sunday School curriculum	1	2	3	4

Questionnaire

4. Below are several statements about SonGames. Please indicate how much you agree with each statement and also include your comments. If the statement does not apply to you, please write N/A. (1=disagree strongly; 4=agree strongly)

DISAGREE   AGREE

1 2 3 4   I liked the Bible theme based on God's team in action. _____
1 2 3 4   Kids of all ages enjoyed SonGames 2004. _____
1 2 3 4   The Bible story review games, Bible memory verse activities and/or SonGames Training Center activities were effective in reinforcing the Bible lesson. _____
1 2 3 4   The lesson format was easy to use. _____
1 2 3 4   Each Bible story and application was relevant to kids' lives. _____
1 2 3 4   Children enjoyed learning from the student guidebooks. _____
1 2 3 4   The Teaching and Decorating Resources visual aids were colorful and helped the children understand each Bible story. _____
1 2 3 4   *Gold-Medal Crafts for Kids* craft book had many fun, useful ideas. _____
1 2 3 4   SonGames songs were fun, catchy and appropriate. _____
1 2 3 4   *Director's Guidebook* made organizing VBS easier. _____
1 2 3 4   The theme posters appealed to adults and children. _____
1 2 3 4   The T-shirt iron-on was attractive and worked well. _____
1 2 3 4   Each day's skit helped children understand the lesson. _____

How did you use the *Teaming Up at SonGames Skit Video*?
❏ Showed video to students _____
❏ Viewed video for acting and staging tips, but performed skits live _____
❏ Did not use skits or video.

5. What would you like to add, change or omit from Gospel Light's Vacation Bible School materials?
   _____
   _____
   _____
   _____

6. Approximately how many children attended your VBS this year? _____

7. How many years has your church used Gospel Light's VBS
   ❑ First year
   ❑ 2 years
   ❑ 3 years
   ❑ 4 years
   ❑ 5+ years

8a. Who in your church decides which VBS curriculum to purchase?
   ❑ Pastor
   ❑ Minister of Education
   ❑ Children's Director
   ❑ Committee
   ❑ VBS Director

   VBS curriculum. (For example, if by committee, give titles of those involved.)
   _____
   _____

9. How did you schedule your VBS program? (Please check all that apply.)
   ❑ 5 consecutive days
   ❑ 2 consecutive weeks
   ❑ 5 consecutive evenings
   ❑ Other (please explain)
   _____

10. After using Gospel Light's VBS this year, would you consider using Gospel Light again next year?
    ❑ Yes   ❑ No

11a. What children's Sunday School curriculum does your church use? _____

    curriculum?
    ❑ Less than 1 year
    ❑ 2-3 years
    ❑ 4-5 years
    ❑ 5+ years

    Sunday School departments?
    ❑ Less than 50
    ❑ 51-100
    ❑ 101-200
    ❑ 201-300
    ❑ 300+

12. Where do you usually buy your Christian education supplies?
    ❑ Bookstore
    ❑ Denominational supplier
    ❑ Curriculum publisher
    ❑ Other (please specify) _____

❑ Yes, I want to review Gospel Light's Sunday School Curriculum. Please send free samples for the following age levels:
   ❑ 2- & 3-year-olds
   ❑ 4- & 5-year-olds
   ❑ Grades 1 & 2 (Primary)
   ❑ Grades 3 & 4 (Middler)
   ❑ Grades 5 & 6 (Junior)

Please send information about:
   ❑ Gospel Light Youth Curriculum
   ❑ Gospel Light Adult Curriculum

Thank you again for your comments. Please fold form so that the address below is on the outside, tape to secure and drop in the mail.

— — FOLD — — — —

BUSINESS REPLY MAIL
FIRST-CLASS MAIL PERMIT 51 VENTURA, CA

POSTAGE WILL BE PAID BY ADDRESSEE

Gospel Light
P.O. BOX 3875
Ventura, CA 93006

Attn: Children's Curriculum/VBS and Resources

No postage necessary if mailed in the United States